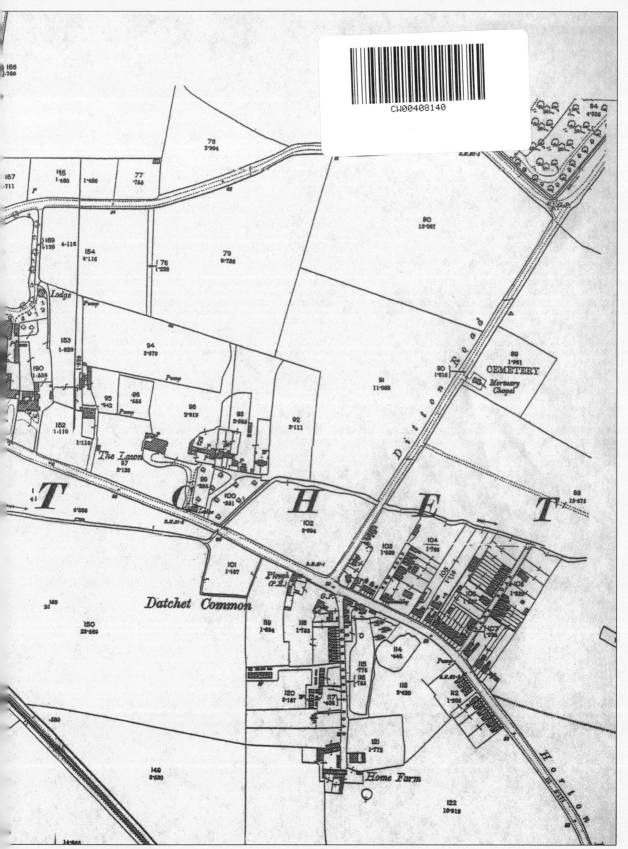

1899 Ordnance Survey map, Victorian development in the village centre and on the Common.

DATCHET
PAST

Aerial views of floods, 1947 (*Daily Graphic*)

DATCHET PAST

Janet Kennish

Phillimore

1999

Published by
PHILLIMORE & CO. LTD.
Shopwyke Manor Barn, Chichester, West Sussex

© Janet Kennish, 1999

ISBN 1 86077 103 3

Printed and bound in Great Britain by
BIDDLES LTD.
Guildford, Surrey

*For Jim and Anne Gautrey,
my late father and my mother*

Contents

Acknowledgements

I am greatly indebted to many people for their contributions to this book. Chiefly among them are Dr. Judith Hunter, for her valuable comments on the manuscript, Chris Kennish for his computer graphic enhancement of many maps and photographs, and Ronald Lewin for proof-reading.

The staff of many record offices and archive collections have been generous with their time and assistance, including those at Aylesbury, Northampton, Beaulieu, and St George's Chapel Windsor, and at the libraries of Eton College and Windsor Castle. Slough Museum, Slough Reference Library and the Museum Collection of the Royal Borough of Windsor and Maidenhead have provided help with many enquiries. Much of my research has depended on access to local records kindly given to me by the Barker Bridge House Trustees, Datchet Parish Council, St Mary's Parish Church and Datchet St Mary's C. of E. school.

Without the work of Datchet Village Society's Fieldwalking Group, led by Emma Sharman, there would hardly have been a chapter on prehistory. I appreciate the hard work which led to their discoveries at the important Southlea site, recorded here in its preliminary stages. Nigel Berryman, the farmer, is especially thanked for his tolerance and enthusiasm for the project, Phil Catherall for his professional interest, and Crown Estates for their help and co-operation.

I owe thanks to the following individuals for information, advice and support: Dr. Jeremy Burchardt, Sarah Collins, Jo Cormier, Hester Davenport, Elizabeth Davies, Philip Dudden, Eric Fernie, Geoffrey Fisher, Dick and Jill Greenaway, Sarah Large, Philip and Mavis Harris, Desmond Hawtrey, Dr. Michael Hoskins, Stephen Heywood, Peter Kennish, James Kinross, Luke Over, Mrs. Rawlings, Brenda Sanctuary, Marion Scarr, Robert Spicer, Angela Tuddenham, David Yates.

Perhaps the most deserving of my thanks are all those people in Datchet who have allowed me access to their houses, their photographs and their memories. I apologise for lack of space to name them all, but hope that some at least will recognise their contributions to this book.

List of Illustrations

Frontispiece: Aerial view of floods, 1947

Illustration Acknowledgements

The following have given their permission to reproduce illustrations: Lionel Hathaway, frontispiece, 11, 106, 111; Crown Copyright/MOD, the Controller of HMSO, 1; Berkshire Archaeological Publications, 2; Royal Borough Windsor and Maidenhead Museum Collection, 3; Reading Museum (Reading Borough Council), 4; Provost and Fellows of Eton College, 6; Bucks & Berks Observer Group, 7, 48; Harry Margary Maps, Lympne, 8; V & A Picture Library, 9; C.A. Lubbock, *The Herschel Chronicle*, CUP, 1933, 54; St Mary's Datchet PCC, 12, 32, 58, 71, 83, 84; Dr. Ian Keen, 14, 17, 65, 78-80, 85, 92-4, 97, 98, 100, 104, 113; County Records and Local Studies Service, Aylesbury, 15, 35, 47; J.A. Pearson, 19, 22-4, 38-40, 42, 43; Ashmolean Museum, Oxford, 21; Lord Montagu of Beaulieu, 26; © The British Museum, 36; Conway Library, Courtauld Institute of Art, 27-31, 49, 59; British Library, 57, 72, 81; Royal Collection Trust, 37; Bodleian Library, Oxford, 41 (MS.Top.gen.a.11, fol. 16, no. 62) © Crown Copyright, RCHME, 51, 64; William Herschel Museum, Bath, 55; Cambridge University Press, 54; *Windsor Express*, 61; B.J.B. Corden, 62, 63; James Kinross, 66-8; Mrs. Sarah Large, dustjacket, 45, 69; Oxfordshire Archives, 82; County Archivist, Reading, and St Mary's C. of E. School, 86-8; Dick Carter, 92; National Motor Museum, 95; T.E.B. Sopwith, 96; Ron and Brenda Lewin, 99; Reg Cleversley, 101; Tom Joyce, 103; Mike Hill, 91, 105, 108; Mrs. Queenie Sams, 107, 109, 114; Frederick Pegg, 110, 112, 115; Bucks County Council, 117; Datchet parish map, surveyed 1997 (Reproduced from 1999 Landplan 1:10,000 scale map by permission of Ordnance Survey on behalf of The Controller of Her Majesty's Stationery Office, © Crown Copyright Licence No. MC 027955).

I would like to thank the following for the photography: Raymond Nicholls, 12, 38-40, 45, 62, 63, 69, 71, 83, 84; Chris Kennish, 5, 32; Tony Clemens, 50; Pam Marsden, 3; *Slough Observer*, 7, 48; I would finally like to thank Chris Kennish for the graphic enhancement to pictures, 2, 8, 15, 20, 26, 37, 47, 58, 77, 86-88, 110, 119.

Preface

In writing this book, I am very aware that it is not possible to reconstruct *the* history of Datchet, only *a* history. So much depends upon the records which have survived and the researcher's interpretation of them. Evidence is not particularly good for Datchet's past, compared with what is available for many other places, and the vast jigsaw puzzle of both place and time has many missing pieces.

There have been several previous histories of the village which have acted as my springboard, in particular that written by Samuel Osborn in 1886. He was able to record not only what he himself knew to be true but also the oral traditions of the time which stretched back several generations earlier. Most of the well known stories about Datchet have their written origin in his history and many of his statements can be corroborated by evidence from other sources.

In this century it is Mr. Edward Page, long-serving school master and parish councillor, to whom I owe the most. Although he did not attempt a complete history of the village he did write several pamphlets about various aspects of its past which demonstrate what an astute and thorough historian he was. He also saw and recorded details from original documents which were still available in the 1920s but which have since disappeared.

More recently, Felix Gameson wrote *The Changing Village* which drew on Osborn's and Page's work and took the research a little further. His was the first reference I came across to Datchet's manor court rolls, which have proved to be one of the richest sources of original records, although one of the most problematic to read and interpret.

It was another school teacher, Philip Parsons, who unknowingly led me 12 years ago to my current obsession. He gave me access to the village school's deeds and log books which date from 1844, and from then there was no turning back. Once the history of the school was published I launched into the wider field of the village, its people and its buildings. This book is the culmination of the first 12 years' work. It endeavours to show how the past has shaped this place where we live now, and how traces of the past can be read in the present.

Although I was not born in Datchet myself, I do have roots here. My great-grandmother and great aunt lived in Montagu Road from 1933 to 1956 and I was brought here to visit as a small child. My clearest memory is of playing on what then seemed a vast expanse, but which I now know to be a small strip, of grassy riverfront. My great-grandmother's grave is in the 'new' cemetery, where my father, an inspiring school teacher and historian, is also now buried.

JANET KENNISH
1999

Subscription List

Martin Abrams
Mr. Dennis G. Allen
Derek Allen
Eve Anderson
Peter Ashford
Barker family
Eileen Barnes
Margaret Barrett
Dr. Wendy Beard
Lord Montagu of Beaulieu
Hilaire Benbow, M.B.E., D.S.C.
Joanne Bence
Mr. M.C.P. Bennett
Angela Hazel Berry
Nigel A. Berryman
Dr. R.G.H. Bethel
Mr. David W. Boss
Margaret Boothman
Kate and Tony Bradbury
Jan Bradstreet and family
Alan Brown
Buckinghamshire Records and Local Studies Service
Brenda Winifred Burdall (née Lewin)
David and Margaret Burditt
Eugene Burden
Arthur Butler
Angus Cameron
Muriel Carter
Mr. Paul Clarke
Philip Clarke
Mr. and Mrs. A.P. Clemens
Michael B.N. Clements
Jonathan Coiley
Miss Marion Coles
Mary and Eric Cook
Sue Cook
Gillian Crane
D. Critchley-Salmonson
Brian T. Cunliffe
Andrew and Lorraine Cunningham
Jeffrey Curtiss
Maggie and Peter Darban
Iris Davies
Penny and Barry Davies
Garrick Davis Esq.

Colin Day
Terry and Jessie Dearle
Ruby L. Dedman
Mrs. Anne Disney
Phillip Dudden
Lucinda Duffy
John Dunford
Mr. C.E. Dyte
Antony Edwards
E.W. Elliott
Les and Shelley Elliott
Mark Antony Ellis
Ronald Emett
Eve Finn
Alan Fletcher
Nick, Maggie, Niamh and Jamie Foster
Margaret Frewin
Roger Frewin
Tony Frewin
Dr. Lewis D.M. Gavin
Brenda Gordon
Craig R. Gordon
Martin D. Gordon
Rob Gordon
David and Alison Green
Tony Griffiths
Miss D.M. Griggs
Roger and Beryl Grime
Leslie Grout
Mrs. Jan Gutteridge
Jane Carruthers Hall
Mr. and Mrs. Hallesy
Neville R. Hamilton
Kathleen R. Hammerson
L.H. Harris
Philip and Mavis Louise Harris
L.B.L. Harwood and J.S. Burnett
Nancy E. Holmes
Alison Hough
Gwenna Howard
Frances Howlett
Ron Hudson
Marion Humphrey
Mr. and Mrs. J.S. and M.J. Hutson
Barbara and David Jefferson

Helen Jenkins
Richard T.C. Jensen
Peter Johnson, BLHA
Hilary Anne Stockley Jones
Robert L.F. Jones
Christopher R. Keeley
Peter Kerfoot
David and Debbi Kemp
Peter and Janet Kennedy
Kirstin King
Houseboat Kingfisher
James Kinross
Kathleen and Geoffrey Knight
Gaynor Koss
Mark Kukla
Darren Laverty
Mrs. E.M. Leafe
Sylvia Rose Lee (née Mower)
Ian Leishman
A.J. Lewin
Joan Lewis
Ronald Harvey Lewin
Teresa and Gavin Livingstone
David and Julie Lloyd
Fiona Loftus
Mr. F.W. Lynn
Ruth MacGillivray
Betty Mann
Mr. and Mrs. L. Manton
Rob Matthews
Christie McGill
Mr. and Mrs. J.F. McWhor
Bill and Sonya Middlemass
C. Mildenhall
Brian G. Mills
Gordon Mills
D.A.R. Mines
Wilfred Morris
William Morris
Sarah Olympia Morshead
Gordon R. Murray
Susan Nixon
Michael Oakes
Tim and Paddy O'Brien
Tim and Linda O'Flynn
Gerry Oliver
Matthew Oliver
Val and Alan Oliver
Rosalind Packham
Kevin Payne
Rod and Pat Peirson
Anne Penfold
George Phillips
Samantha Philo
Ron and Janet Piggott

Alan G. Pope
Poz
Mr. and Mrs. I. Pudney
Jonnathan Ramsay
Rosanna Ramsay
Rupert Ramsay
Patricia Reader
Rishbeth family
Mr. and Mrs. A.V. Roach
David and Pauline Roberts
Mrs. J. Robinson
Pam Robinson
Katherine Rogers
Royal Borough Museum Collection
Rural History Centre, University of Reading
Queenie Sams
Brenda Sanctuary
Ronald Schafer
Audrey M. Scott
Mrs. Emma Scott
Brenda Smith
Les Smith
Aleck and Noemia Stacey
Mr. Peter Stevens
Beryl Hazel Foreman Stickland
Graham George Stickland
Jo Stickland
Paul Russell Stickland
Janet Stocks
Mr. and Mrs. D.J. Street and family
John and Barbara Street, Nicola and Susan
Bill Sullivan
Mrs. Dorothy Taylor
Norman Taylor
Mrs. Audrey Thomas
Mr. A. Thompson
William R.J. Thompson
John Townend
Miss A.M. Tuddenham
Peggy Turner
Paul and Sonya Verbecke
Jean and Ian Wagstaff
Maggie Waller
Roger Walmsley
Sophie Walsh
Amanda Ward
John Warren
Joanne Watt (née Webster)
Mary W. Wenham (née Gillett)
Roy West
Percy Whitford
The Dean and Canons of Windsor
Mr. and Mrs. D. Wooden
Joe Young

The author and publisher wish to acknowledge generous sponsorship towards production costs from the following companies and to thank them for their support of this project.

Chapter One

The Riverside Settlement:
Prehistoric Times

The story of Datchet starts with the River Thames. Its wide flood plain was formed at the end of the Ice Ages, with gravel and silt being deposited as the melted water moved south, and floods still threaten to engulf the crops, roads and homes of the people living alongside it Although the river itself is now confined to a single narrow channel, in prehistoric times there were multiple streams meandering along a wider and flatter course which has shifted over many thousands of years.

From the Mesolithic period, between 10,000 and 6,500 years ago, there is evidence of people living in the area which was to become Datchet. These people did not settle for long in any one place, but they certainly passed through here, fishing and hunting with flint tools, of which about twenty have been found during dredging in the Thames. Several Mesolithic flint axe heads have also been dug up from gardens in Castle Avenue. From about 6,500 years ago groups of Neolithic people were moving through the country, making a much greater impact on the landscape. They built stone circles and tombs, cleared forests and cultivated fields. Again, their flint tools have been retrieved from the river bed: around thirty flint or stone axes and blades, some of fine workmanship.

The first real evidence of a settled village at Datchet comes from the Bronze Age between 4,400 to 2,700 years ago, when technological revolutions in metal working arrived from the continent. Excavations at nearby Runnymede, and more recently at the Eton rowing trench and Maidenhead flood relief channel, are building up a picture of organised and extensive riverside villages and farming communities along the banks of the Thames from about 1500 B.C. Investigation has also recently begun into a complex prehistoric site at Southlea Farm, just south of Datchet. It was first identified from aerial photographs, taken during drought years, which reveal cropmarks where prehistoric disturbance beneath the soil has caused the crop to grow more or less vigorously. The site is on an 'island' of high ground centred close to Southlea Farm and extending into the cropmark field. This area remains dry even in major floods and is thus a likely place for an early village to have been established. The results of a geophysics survey suggest that the present hedge and ditch on the southern edge of the field may still follow the same line as the boundary of the prehistoric settlement. Beyond the next field, towards the Thames, there is a long thin strip of alluvial soil which may represent one of the many 'paleo-channels' of the river's previous course. Since then, the Thames has shifted further south to its present deep loop, so that the prehistoric site was probably much closer to the river bank than it is now.

The most noticeable features on the aerial photos are four large circular features, almost

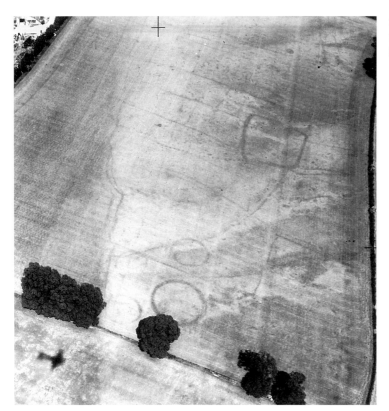

1 Aerial photograph, taken in 1957, showing cropmarks at Southlea Farm.

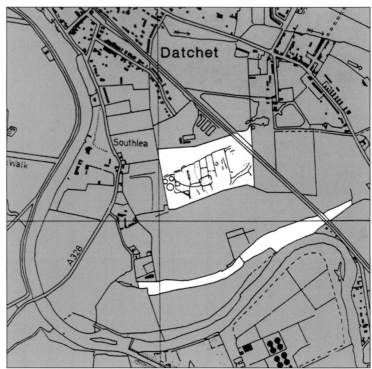

2 Location of cropmarks at Southlea, plotted by Timothy Gates, 1975. The main concentration of cropmarks is highlighted, and also a possible paleo-channel of the Thames to the south.

certainly the remains of Bronze-Age burial
mounds (barrows), which have been completely
flattened by ploughing. It is typical of sites in
the Thames Valley that there should be either
two or four such barrows in a group, and this
cemetery may represent the earliest use of the
site, from between 2500 to 1500 B.C. Current
opinion suggests that the grid-like field system
laid out as strips of remarkably regular width
with subdivisions across their lengths, migh have
its origins in the Bronze-Age period but with
further development some centuries late in the
Iron Age.[1] Once burials had been made, the
site would have remained significant for future
generations who are likely to have lived nearby

the barrows but without obliterating them.
The aerial photos also show several tracks or
droveways and a row of pits which may mark
a boundary fence, all overlaying each other in
complex ways, with a large rectangular
enclosure and a less clearly marked smaller one.

The enclosures are likely to have
contained dwelling huts, animal shelters,
working areas and a rubbish dump or midden.
The technique of fieldwalking, systematically
collecting surface material turned up by the
plough, is producing an impressive amount of
prehistoric pottery and flint. In 1998, the first
year of fieldwalking, most of the pottery
fragments were found near the enclosure. While

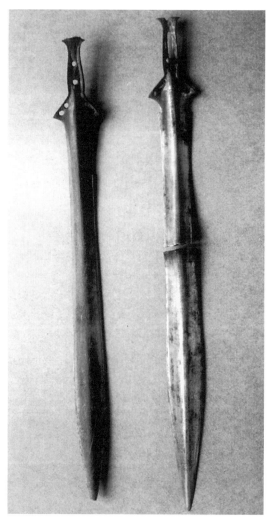

3   A middle Bronze-Age axe-head, or palstave,
dredged from the Thames in 1870.

4   Two late Bronze-Age swords (one broken, perhaps
deliberately in antiquity), dating from around 900
B.C., found in 1982 during gravel extraction at
Kingsmead in the Welley field, now Wraysbury parish.

5 Pottery sherds found on surface of the field at Southlea.

(a)   *Above left.* Incised and shaped rim and body fragment, early Iron Age;

(b)   *Above right.* Incised and impressed decoration, early Iron Age;

(c)   *Below.* Rim fragments, Iron Age, Roman on far right.

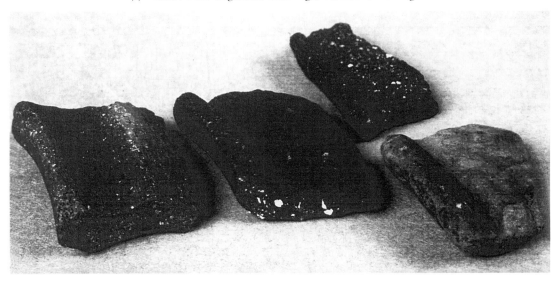

a full assessment is still to be carried out, a first opinion suggests that much of the pottery dates from the Iron Age, particularly the earlier part of the period, from about 700 B.C. but also through to the Romano-British first centuries A.D.[2] A number of pieces are decorated with finger-tip impressions and incised or impressed patterns which should eventually allow firmer dating to be made in comparison with pottery from other local sites. A quantity of flint scrapers and blades is also being collected, and these are likely to date from the Bronze-Age phase of settlement. However, the discovery of one tiny worked flint about a centimetre long, a Meso-lithic 'microlith', suggests that this site could have been inhabited, perhaps temporarily, by the most ancient hunter-gathering people. Most recently, a large and intact quernstone was found, by the same sharp-eyed fieldwalker who spotted the microlith. It is in extrememly good condition and has been identified as coming from a known quern production site at Lodsworth in Sussex, from where they were distributed across the region and especially along river routes.[3] It is dateable to the Iron-Age period, not later than the first century B.C. The whole Southlea site has been described as a rare and intact prehistoric landscape,[4] and investigations will continue there under the guidance of professionals but with continuing community involvement.

During the Bronze Age, the new metal would at first only have been available for privileged members of society, used mainly for weapons and melted down for re-working rather than discarded, but, as the supply increased, tools and jewellery were also made. Dredging in the Thames near Datchet has

recovered more than thirty objects from the Middle and Late Bronze Age, including spear and axe heads, daggers, blades and swords. Some must be the result of accidental loss or drowning, but it is also possible that the dead were disposed of in rivers, along with their possessions. However, because such a large number of Bronze-Age artefacts have been found concentrated at river sites, it is thought that valued objects were ritually sacrificed by being thrown into the river as offerings to the gods. Many of the Datchet finds are likely to have been such ritual sacrifices. From about 600 B.C., iron was introduced into Britain by Celtic traders and settlers, gradually replacing bronze for weapons and tools, though the softer metal was still used for decorative objects.

6 Celtic brooch dredged from the Thames. Now in the Myers collection, Eton College.

7 A quernstone, the top one of two for grinding corn, found at the Southlea site. It was made, of greensand stone, at Lodsworth in Sussex in the first or second century B.C.

The most exceptional river find is a splendid and unusual bronze brooch, which was dredged from the Thames in the 1870s and is now in the Myers Collection at Eton College. About four inches long, it is bow shaped, and decorated with beads of amber and blue glass, all nine of which have survived. The point of its pin is protected in the same way as a modern safety pin, a typical device of the time which was not re-invented until many centuries later. It dates from the late Iron Age, around 100 B.C. to A.D. 100, during the period of Celtic culture in Britain which produced extremely sophisticated decorative metalwork. The Datchet brooch was a luxury object produced by highly skilled craftsmen, and must have belonged to someone of élite social status.

The place name 'Datchet' is agreed by experts to be of Celtic origin, which is unusual in an area where most place names are Saxon or later in date. The word itself is not thought have any descriptive meaning, although an earlier theory was that the 'cet' element referred to woodland.[5] The British, or Celtic, tribes remained in their homelands under the rule of the Roman occupation, but retreated from most of southern Britain during the waves of Saxon invasion in the fifth and sixth centuries A.D. The Roman period, from the first to the late fourth centuries A.D., has left little trace locally except for a sprinkling of finds around Slough and Windsor. Only a few pieces of Roman pottery and one coin have been found so far in Datchet, although the Southlea site may prove to have been inhabited during the Romano-British period as well. The Celtic origin of 'Datchet' demonstrates that a village called by that name existed here before the time of the Saxon invasions, and it is possible that there has been continuous habitation here for up to five thousand years.

The Southlea site is 'visible' to us as cropmarks because its traces were left relatively undisturbed in the fields near Southlea Farm (which is itself on the high 'island' and dates from medieval times), but such evidence is lost where a village site remains in use. It is known that villages were often moved within a community's home territory, so the present nucleus of Datchet could be either a later resettlement or an anciently inhabited alternative centre. The watercourse which runs through the middle of Datchet, now culverted underground, is probably another paleo-channel of the Thames whose main course eventually became settled just a short distance away. As at Southlea, there is a significant island of high ground which became the focus for safe and dry dwellings, now represented by the church and churchyard.

Chapter Two

Ferry and Manor: Medieval Period

The Saxons, the Normans and Domesday Book

The first known written reference to Datchet occurs in a document dated about the year 994, in King Elthelred's reign. This charter records the exchange of land owned in 'Deccet' by Wynflaed for other lands in Berkshire owned by Aelfric, but gives no information beyond the fact of Datchet's existence as a place. The actual spelling of the name varies in written sources until very recent times, as writers interpreted the sounds they heard; from the Saxon Deccet, Norman Daceta, through Detchet and Dotchet, Datchette and Dotchatt. These and other variations are not consistent and do not indicate any significant change in the name throughout the centuries.

There was an Anglo-Saxon settlement of major significance nearby at Old Windsor, situated on the Berkshire bank of the Thames, in an area which later became Kingsbury (King's town) Field. Its origins go back to about A.D. 600, with a great expansion between the years 750 and 850. A huge water mill was built then, and a long mill channel from the river was dug across a loop of the Thames. By the 1040s 'Windsores' was a royal residence, when Edward the Confessor was recorded as healing the blind in the royal palace of Windsor. From 1080 the castle at 'New Windsor' was being built and the Saxon town eventually became known as 'Old Windsor'. Datchet's Celtic name did not change during the Saxon period, implying that it was not re-founded at this time. With the chief Saxon focus at Old Windsor, the village would have been just one among many minor riverside settlements, and possibly one of several places where there was a ford across the Thames. The later written records of many Old English (i.e. Anglo Saxon) field names make it quite clear that the community was well established in this early period.

In common with the majority of villages in England, it is Domesday Book which gives the first account of Datchet in any detail. This survey, conducted in 1085–86, was an inventory and valuation of land, and a record of its owners after King William had distributed the possessions of the old Anglo-Saxon nobility to the conquering Normans. It was drawn up for tax assessment purposes and also to establish rightful ownership in case of dispute in the future.

The new owners took over the land and its organisation much as it had been structured before the Conquest. The fundamental unit of local landholding and administration was already the manor, and it was the manor which was recorded in Domesday Book. A manor is a difficult concept to define, but implies an estate held by a lord over which he had jurisdiction, and whose tenants were bound to him by right. In the case of Datchet, the size and shape of the later parish probably corresponds quite closely to that of the original manor. The manorial system was based on the assumption that all land was ultimately owned by the king. He had the right to give it as he pleased, and military service was owed to him in return. He could also revoke the gift if the recipient displeased him. Tenants owed service to their lord and through him to the king. The great landowners held manors in many different parts of England and their ownership conferred military power, as in time of strife they had the right to call up for armed service all those who owed them allegiance. Later, actual service was replaced by money dues or supply of produce, so that the possession of a manor, or a clutch of manors, was a financial asset and a basis for power.

This is the Domesday text for Datchet in a modern translation,[1] followed by an explanation for each itemised section:

1   Giles brother of Ansculf holds DATCHET (Daceta) for 13 ½ hides.
2   Land for 12 ploughs; in lordship 5 hides; 1 plough there;   4 ploughs possible.
3   16 villagers with 6 smallholders have 7 ploughs; 3 slaves.
4   Meadow for 5 ploughs; woodland, 300 pigs; 2 fisheries 2,000 eels.
5   The total value is and was £6; before 1066 £12.
6   Saewulf, Earl Leofwin's man, held 6 hides and 3 virgates of this manor as one manor; his brother Siward, Earl Harold's man, also held 6 hides and 3 virgates; they could sell their land.

1   Also known as Giles de Pinkeni. A hide was the amount of land which could be ploughed by one ox team in a year, perhaps about 120 acres, sufficient to support a household.
2   The five hides 'in Lordship' was land farmed by the lord himself or his tenant, which was known as the demesne of the manor.
3   Villagers (or villeins) were the peasants who held most land, while the smallholders (or bordars) held less. All were 'tied' to the manor and were obliged to plough the lord's land as well as their own. Slaves worked entirely for the lord, but later they merged with the classes of peasant landholders. The numbers given are heads of households or families, though the three slaves were probably individuals, so the population of the manor seems to have consisted of about twenty-two families.
4   Datchet was rich in meadow land lying alongside the river on the south and west, and by the streams on the north and east. Pigs were fed by letting them forage in woodland. The two fisheries were probably at Black Potts on the northern boundary and near Albert Bridge to the south, where they continued to operate until early this century.
5   The value of the manor was an estimate of the total income its lord would receive annually in money and in produce from his peasants. A higher value before the Conquest in 1066 is not at all unusual and may be due to the disruption of the Conquest itself.
6   Saewulf and Siward were both nobles under the defeated King Harold and still held parts of of Datchet as sub-tenants which was not unusual. A virgate was a quarter of a hide.

Although it seems odd, Fulmer was then owned together with Datchet. A survey of the manor taken in 1254 makes it clear that the main areas of woodland were in Fulmer rather than in Datchet itself. This reflects a pattern common in south Buckinghamshire, where parishes tend to be aligned north-south in a long thin shape, crossing the various river terraces to give each parish (or originally the manor) a share of each different type of soil. Woodland in particular is often separated by some distance to the north of the main settlement. The 1254 survey also shows how land tenancy had changed since Domesday, with direct service beginning to be replaced by hired labour, as freehold tenants paying rents are recorded as well as land worked by villagers. By this date there were also 12 cottagers, without land of their own. Already the structure of the manorial community was changing, reflecting the national pattern of diminishing power of feudal lordships by the late 13th century.

Medieval Manors: Ditton, Datchet, Riding

Giles, brother of Ansculf, the Norman owner of Datchet, was one of the Conqueror's great landowners; his main residence was at Weedon in Northamptonshire, though he owned 15 other manors. Giles was related to the even more powerful William FitzAnsculf (son of Ansculf), who in 1086 had a castle at Dudley as well as 30 manors in Buckinghamshire and Berkshire. These included both Stoke Poges and Ditton, whose future history was to be closely intertwined with that of Datchet.

Giles' family name was de Pinkney, from Picquigny in the Somme; one of the new foreign ruling class rewarded by William for their part in his success. Mostly these great men must have been absentee lords of many of their smaller manors, where only the steward would have been in charge. For the peasant classes who worked the land, a change of over-lord probably made little difference to their lives. The Normans generally adopted the local customs, and management of the land continued much as it had been before the Conquest.

The de Pinkney family owned Datchet for another 250 years, until the 1330s, but not without difficulties. England was in an almost constant state of conflict among king and nobles; property was frequently confiscated as a punishment and redistributed as a reward. During the rebellion against King John in 1216, Robert de Pinkney's estates were seized, but returned to him when he was pardoned by the next king, Henry III.

In the early 14th century, Datchet changed hands several times, becoming a pawn in the quarrels between King Edward II and factions opposing him. Some time before 1300, Henry de Pinkney granted Datchet, without royal permission, to a colourful character called Hugh le Despenser the Elder. Both he and his son, Hugh the Younger, were royal officials, and Hugh the Younger was reputed to be Edward II's lover after the death of his first

favourite, Piers Gaveston. Fabulously wealthy, the Despensers' centre of power was in the Welsh borders, and both father and son represented a challenge to the king's authority. In 1326, after treasonable involvement in a conspiracy against the king, both were hanged and Hugh the Younger was also drawn and quartered. After their downfall, their lands were forfeited to the king and Datchet Manor was returned in 1331 to Edmund de Pinkney for life, though he died in 1332.

On the death of Edmund de Pinkney, King Edward III leased the Manor of Datchet to the de Molyns family, who already owned Ditton and Stoke Poges. There are brasses and a tomb commemorating later members of the de Molyns family in Stoke Poges church. John de Molyns was granted a licence to fortify the manor houses at Stoke and Ditton in 1335. A royal licence was required by a noble wanting to do this, in case such a stronghold was used as a base from which to oppose the king. The castle tower built at Ditton became known as the de Molyns Tower, and was said still to have been in existence in 1812 when Ditton House was destroyed by fire. Also in 1335, John de Molyns was granted a licence to create a deer park at Ditton, taking in land from Datchet, which was further enlarged in 1338 by the addition of land belonging to Langley. He also established private chantry chapels at Stoke Poges and Ditton, and in 1921 a beautiful bronze figure from a medieval crucifix was dug up from the ground at Ditton Park just a short distance from the present rebuilt chapel.

Between the village of Datchet and the boundary of Ditton Park to its north east there was another substantial estate called Riding, later Riding Court. This came into John de Molyns' possession at the same time as Stoke Poges, and he was granted Right of Free Warren there in 1331. This was a privilege under the king's control, allowing the holder to keep small game for hunting: pheasant, partridge, hare and rabbit. These last were

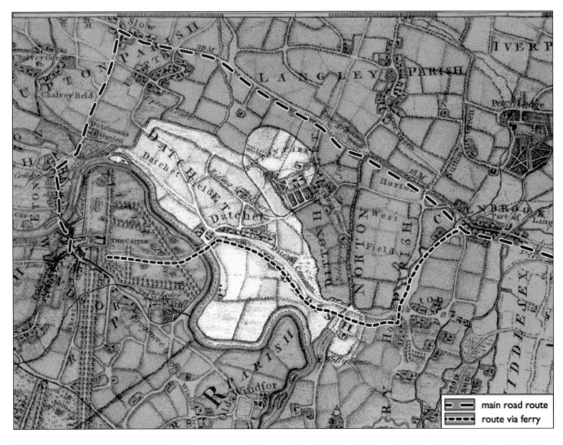

8   Datchet, Ditton Park and Riding Court based on Rocque's map of Berkshire, 1761. The parish of Datchet and Ditton Park are highlighted. It can be seen that almost the whole length of the parish boundary is defined by water, as river or streams.

9   Bronze figure from a crucifix found near the chapel at Ditton Park in 1921, dating from the late 1300s or early 1400s.

introduced to England in Norman times and were bred in 'warrens', only becoming wild in the late 18th and 19th centuries. In the 1830s, a small field north of Riding Court house was still named 'The Warren' and is very likely to indicate a medieval warren site. Riding is first mentioned in a deed of 1196, by which Ralf de Rudinges sold land in Rudinges. The name derives from the Anglo-Saxon 'hryding', meaning a clearing in woodland. During the late 12th century more land was being brought under cultivation to feed a growing population, and the shape of the fields around the house suggests that the boundaries have been pushed outward from the focus of a new settlement. The house with its extensive farm buildings has been rebuilt several times, but probably on the original medieval site.

The right to hold a fair in meadows near Datchet was granted to John de Molyns in 1335, this being a privilege because the Lord would profit from the event. A fair in medieval times was an extension of a market, bringing large crowds of people and a wide range of traders selling goods not normally available, and they were usually granted to places where a weekly market was already held. Fairs often took place in the summer, when travelling was easier, and were associated with the village's or town's saint's day. In Datchet, it was held on 15 August, the Feast of the Assumption of the Virgin Mary. The last known mention of this fair was in 1438.

Members of the de Molyns family became involved in the bitter disputes for the Crown known as the Wars of the Roses, and two of them were beheaded in the 1460s as Lancastrians. In 1472, under the Yorkist Edward IV, the family was pardoned and given back most of their estates which had previously been confiscated. Fulmer, which had been linked with Datchet, was returned with Stoke Poges to the de Molyns family, but, crucially, Datchet, and Riding and Ditton manors, were kept by the king as his own possessions. Thus events in national history had a lasting effect on the story of Datchet which remained in royal hands until the 17th century.

The Manor of Ditton was centred on the moated and fortified Ditton House, surrounded by Ditton Park and with its chantry chapel, farm and hamlet nestling close by. But until 1472 the Manor of Datchet with Riding was administered from Stoke Poges. After 1472, Riding had 'Court' added to its name for the first time, which means that the manor courts for Datchet were held there from that time. The present Manor House on the south side of Datchet village centre dates from the 16th century, which is also the time from which manor court proceedings for Datchet Manor survive in an almost unbroken sequence.

Castle and Ferry

In the years after the Conquest, William consolidated his control over England by building a series of castles at strategic points, and in particular in a defensive ring round London. Windsor was one of these, a new foundation moving the focus of royal interest from Old Windsor on the riverside to 'New Windsor' on a defensible hill. In the year 1110 King Henry I held his court for the first time in Windsor Castle, and the royal favour in which it was held is shown by the fact that Henry's marriage took place in the castle chapel in 1112. By 1180 much of its defences had been rebuilt in stone, and in 1230 Henry III erected the massive curtain wall with three drum towers.

It is from this period that Datchet ferry is known to have been a significant river crossing as a route to the castle, although it can be assumed to have existed before then. In 1249, Henry III gave a great oak from his royal Windsor forest to build a barge 'to make the passage of Datchet'. The barge needed replacing in 1278, when Edward I ordered 'a great barge for the king's ferry at Datchete' to be made. The implication is that the ferry was a specifically royal route. There was also a bridge across the Thames at Windsor by the 1230s, but for light horse and foot travel the ferry was a shorter and more direct route from the castle, through Datchet and Horton to Colnbrook on the main road towards London.

The valuable rights and profits of the ferry are recorded as belonging to the Manor of Datchet from the 1300s. One of the many records of the de Pinkney family's disputes with the king over their possessions cites: 'Datchete manor including a fishery, with a ferry across the Thames, held of the king by service of a knight's fee and finding two armed footmen in time of war, in the castle of Windsor, for forty days'. Another describes the 'Manor of Datchet, whereof the ferry over the Thames to Windsor is parcel and appurtenant thereto from time out of mind'. (The phrase 'time out of mind', used in a legal sense, referred to the period before Richard I's accession in 1189.) From 1472, when Datchet became a Crown possession, the ownership of the ferry was under royal control.

The inhabitants of the village at this time cannot always have been pleased with their proximity to the castle. In 1276, an enquiry was held into whether Henry de Pinkney had paid the fees he owed for 'castle guard for the Castle of Wyndesor'. He said that he used to pay these dues out of the profits of his various manors around the country, although the payment was actually made at the castle by his steward in Datchet. When the fees were in arrears, he used to 'distrain [collect] in Datchet, because it was nearer the castle'.

Church and Rectory

The network of English parishes and the churches which served them was largely developed by about 1200, although individual churches could have been founded long before then. Parishes were often based on manorial boundaries with the lord providing the church, as seems to be the case at Datchet. A church certainly existed here by the 1150s, when Gilbert de Pinkney, the Lord of the Manor, gave it to the Abbey of St Albans. The abbot,

as rector of the parish, would then have had the right to appoint a vicar as the minister of the church, and this right was confirmed by Henry de Pinkney in 1238. It is from this date that the vicars' names are recorded, the first being Nicholas Greene, who was presented to the living in 1239. By 1348 the church had been taken under the direct control of King Edward III, and in 1350 he gave it as part of the endowment of his new chapel and college of St George at Windsor Castle. Datchet church was one of the many properties given by Edward to the chapel, including the churches at Wraysbury and Iver.

Edward III's endowment was a critical factor in the future of Datchet. In much the same way as a manor, the church was worth a precise amount and was part of the wealth and power base of its owners. A parish church was a source of revenue from the tithes payable to it, which were due to the rector officiating in the parish unless the church was controlled by another body in the position of rector—the king, an abbey, a noble, or a college. In this case, the Chapel of St George received the greater or rectorial portion of the tithes, formerly owned by St Albans Abbey. St George's then had the right to appoint a vicar of their choice as clergyman in the church itself, to whom the smaller, vicarial, portion of the tithes was due. The value of the church largely derived from these tithes, theoretically a tenth of all crops, produce, stock and labour of the parish. As they did with many of their possessions, the dean and canons of the chapel 'farmed out', or leased, the collection of the tithe revenues from the parish to a lay middleman. He was called the rector and paid rent for the lands, making a profit from the arrangement. Adding to the confusion, the rector was occasionally the same person as the vicar.

The dean and canons of the chapel, in the role of rector, were responsible for the building and repair of the chancel of the church where the rite of the Mass was conducted, but not for the nave where the common people

10 Floods, in 1891 or '94, outside the parish council shop; next is the Rectory House before it was remodelled, now Old Priory.

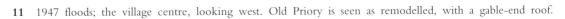

11 1947 floods; the village centre, looking west. Old Priory is seen as remodelled, with a gable-end roof.

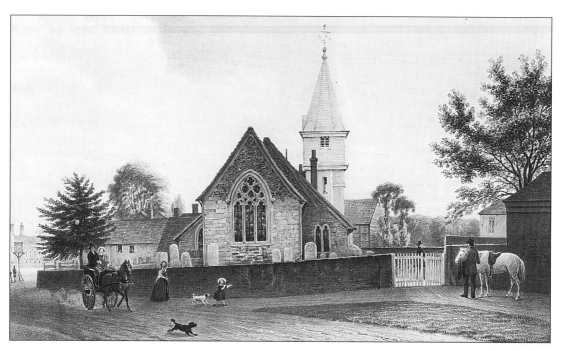

12 St Mary's Church from London Road before rebuilding, by William Corden, 1857. On the far left is Manor House, before remodelling, and Manor Cottages. Just to the left of the church is the *Royal Stag* before the addition of Gothic windows. On the right of the church is the Rectory barn, then the original vicarage, and Datchet House stable. The chimney in the north aisle roof served a fireplace in a private pew.

sat or stood. They carried out rebuilding or a major repair of the chancel in 1367, and minor works frequently after that, but by 1556 the churchwardens reported that the chancel was in a ruinous condition, the fault of the Chapel and College of Windsor. During the time when the church belonged to St Alban's Abbey it is known that the rector owned a house in Datchet, as one was mentioned in a legal dispute in 1290. When the church was given to St George's Chapel, the rectory is known to have been on the site of the house near the church now called Old Priory, and that is probably where it was in 1290. (There never was a priory in Datchet, but there was a 19th-century owner called Mr. Prior, who renamed his house in this most confusing way.)

In 1376 a new house was built 'within the mansion of the Rectory', the term 'mansion' here meaning an official dwelling. It included 'A barn, granary, stable, kitchen

and brewery, all rebuilt at the College's expense by John Milcombe, Vicar and Rector of Datchet'. The house has since been rebuilt several times by wealthy rectors, and nothing now survives from the 14th century. The barn and granary were needed for storing the tithe produce, and part of a very large barn behind the rectory can be seen beyond the church in a view painted in 1857. In 1350 several other properties in Datchet were bought by St George's. These seem to have included the site of the original vicarage just to the north of the church (demolished during the Victorian rebuilding), and possibly that of the present parish drop-in centre, which from Elizabethan times is known to have been a poorhouse under the auspices of the church. The timing of these purchases suggests that it may have been due to the Black Death in 1348-9 that an unusual number of dwellings became available.

St Helen's Manor and Southlea Farm

Another religious institution was also involved in Datchet by the 13th century. The priory, or nunnery, of St Helen's at Bishopgate in London owned a 'farm' at Southlea (in the sense of land rented out), and other properties scattered throughout Datchet. These amounted to a sub-manor called Datchet St Helen's alongside the Manor of Datchet.

At Southlea, between the farm and the river, there are high brick-walled enclosures with a great gateway, decayed but still impressive. It is known that they were substantially repaired in 1817, being the garden walls belonging to a house just to their north which is now demolished. In 1839 a parish map describes them as 'monastery walls', which may suggest the survival of a traditional memory, but they are not referred to by that name in any earlier documents and there was never a religious community here. However, the walls may represent the site of a monastic grange sending produce and rent back to the priory in London. Several fine specimen

trees within the walls are typical of Datchet's late 18th-century gardens, and the bricks themselves appear to be of the same period. There is much local superstition concerning this site, including the tradition of a tunnel going under the river to Windsor Castle. Stories of tunnels are widely spread folklore; the tunnels on investigation usually turn out to be cellars, though in this case a brick drainage channel running into the Thames nearby may be the explanation. St Helen's Priory also owned the large field called Sundermead or Sumptermead, on the riverside north of the village which is now part of the golf course. The original name meant a field separated [sundered] from the main centre, which is exactly the situation in this case.

St Helen's was one of the smaller monasteries dissolved by Henry VIII in 1536, when its properties were sold. As a manor it was absorbed into Datchet, which was from then officially described as The Manor of Datchet with Datchet St Helen's. In surveys, however, its original lands continued to be

13 Eighteenth-century walls at Southlea Farm, near the site of old Southlea House.

14   Looking north along the High Street, 1915; from right: the Post House, Park Villas (built 1850s), Holiman's Plat (a much lower roof level), then Clifton House, The Cottage and Little Dene in the distance.

identified as belonging to Datchet St Helen's Manor. The house in the High Street called Holiman's Plat was until recently known as St Helen's Cottage. It now dates from the 17th and 18th centuries, but its name suggests that it once belonged to the Manor of St Helen's.

The Medieval Village Centre

There is a good deal of evidence to suggest that the earliest settlement was centred on and around the high ground where the church stands, and that the Manor House range on the south side of the village centre watercourse was a later development. The churchyard, roughly oval in shape and circling a defined mound, is typical of a very early fortified enclosure. The high ground would provide a safe refuge from flood, and fortifications would protect against threats from outside.

Among a large collection of deeds related to rectory property in St George's archives is a grant of land by Henry de Pinkney in the mid-1200s. It refers to land 'of the old court', which implies that the manor courts had at one time been held in a building somewhere in this area close to the church. Many other 14th- and 15th-century deeds, are related to properties which clustered around the rectory and churchyard. These are now represented by the *Royal Stag*; the old almshouse ('The Bridge'); the Bank and Bank House, built on land owned by Eton College; and 'Old Priory', originally the rectory. Even on a modern map it can be seen how all these plots of land fit tightly against each other around the focal point of the church. This original centre included medieval predecessors of Datchet House to the north and Church Cottage to the west. In the mid-1970s deep digging during mains services work outside Church Cottage revealed several skeletons buried far below ground level. Although it seems they were neither removed nor recorded, their presence suggests that in the remote past the churchyard included the slope across the road to Church Cottage.

15 Plan of the medieval village centre, based on the 1834 enclosure map.

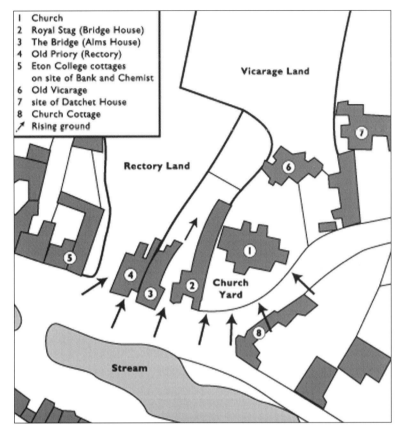

1 Church
2 Royal Stag (Bridge House)
3 The Bridge (Alms House)
4 Old Priory (Rectory)
5 Eton College cottages on site of Bank and Chemist
6 Old Vicarage
7 site of Datchet House
8 Church Cottage
↗ Rising ground

Vicarage Land

Rectory Land

Church Yard

Stream

16 The *Royal Stag*, 15th-century rear bays seen from the churchyard. The gothic-style upper windows are late 19th- or early 20th-century alterations.

The back part of the *Royal Stag* is probably the oldest building in Datchet, with the possible exception of some stonework in the chancel of the church. Seen from the churchyard, there are five timber-framed bays, two at the front as a dwelling place and the three at the rear for housing animals. This building probably dates from the 1400s, when it would have been a hall house, a single-storey room open to the rafters with a central hearth and a hole in the roof for the escape of smoke. Later, probably around 1600, an upper floor and chimney were inserted.

A house existed on the site of Church Cottage before 1330, as in that year it was bought by Adam Wodyat of Datchet. Two hundred years later, the wealthy and prolific Mathewe family owned a property called 'Woodgates Hall' which can be identified with the present house.

The surname 'Wodyat' had become the name of the house, 'Woodgates', due to the sounds for *g* and *y* being interchangeable. The house we know today as Church Cottage is likely to have been rebuilt by John Mathewe in the early 1500s as a hall house; some of its roof timbers are still sooted from an open central fire. It was given an upper floor around 1600 when the tall brick chimney stack was built through the centre of the house and a

staircase was added in the small square projecting front wing. Its timber frame remains remarkably complete and unchanged inside and at the back, although it was probably always plastered over at the front.

To the east of the village centre is another late medieval house, now the three small Astracot cottages. They were originally one rather grand hall house with a two-storey cross wing at the west end, probably built in the early 1500s. All its timber-framed structure is visible inside, though a fashionable brick façade and sash windows were added in the 18th century. It seems to have been one of the properties owned by St George's Chapel in Windsor, perhaps originally a grange farm belonging to the rectory estates.

Fields and Farming

The landscape and the way in which the land was farmed in medieval times are not documented in any early map of the area, but can be reconstructed to some extent from later sources, refer to map on page 21. The first detailed large scale map is the one drawn in 1834, when the great changes in land ownership brought about by enclosure were recorded and described. It can be used as a base to recreate the extent and names of fields from medieval times. The boundaries of the parish

17 Church Cottage, early 16th century (the white building to the left of the shop) seen in an Edwardian postcard. James Cottages and the long wall of Datchet House are seen in the distance on the left.

18 Astracot, Horton Road, 18th-century façade and 20th-century projecting shop front, most recently used as a café.

19 Cottages at Datchet, 18th-century drawing, possibly the Astracot group before the new façade was added. It is known that a projecting wing, such as shown on the left of this building, was reduced back to the level of the remodelled façade.

were probably also anciently established, following either the river or streams for almost the whole of their length. It is only where Datchet meets Wraysbury and Horton near Welley Road that the boundary has been variable, originally including, but now excluding, the Welley field.

We use the term 'field' to mean a privately owned and hedged or fenced plot of farm land, but its original meaning was completely the opposite. An arable field was typically large, open, and communally worked by many owners, while the smaller areas of privately held land were described as a 'close', literally 'enclosed' rather than open. In Datchet, two of these open fields, *Le Lynche* (Linchfield) and

Le Mershe (Marshfield) are recorded in documents from the early 1300s. Two others, Churchfield and Westfield, were named by 1500. Everyone living on the Manor, as owner or tenant, farmed long thin strips of arable distributed throughout the open fields, each farmer's plots being scattered among those of his neighbours. The ploughed strips were grouped in blocks, or furlongs, which were individually named within the fields. The names *Grasfurlong, Thamesfurlong, Westmidefurlong, Morfurlong, Estlongfurlong,* and *Brocfurlong* were recorded in the 1300s. These are Old English place names, showing the typical combination of several elements into one compound word. Most of them refer to the location or shape of the land, but *Ramfurlong* may be derived from the name of John le Ram of Datchet who was killed in 1310, see page 22.

The farming of these holdings, the rotation of crops and fallow land and the pasturing of animals depended upon communal organisation administered through the manor courts. Ownership or tenancy of land in the open fields also carried rights of pasture on fallow land and after harvest, when the fields were thrown open to a regulated number of sheep and cattle for each landholder, both to feed on the stubble and to manure the land.

Meadow land was also needed for growing hay, opened as communal pasture after hay-making. Datchet was rich in water meadows, both near the Thames and on the parish boundaries watered by Mead Brook and Fleet Brook. In *Northmed* (Northmead), on the northern boundary, some Old English plot names are known: *Wilbaldesham, Waterihale, Balmerescroft, Grumbardesdol* and *Halfeyerdedel.* The last two incorporate the word element *dol*, showing that the land was shared out annually, so that *Halfeyerdedel* means 'half year dole'. The great Fleet meadow, *La Flete*, is the earliest field name yet found in Datchet, recorded in 1253. The name has two possible derivations, both from Old English; one from *fleot*, a stream (the Fleet Brook runs round it into the Thames), or from its position on the parish boundary, and the word *geflit*, 'land in dispute'. The Mirk (or Merk) place name may also derive from being on a border, in this case with Upton, as *mearc* meant land on a boundary, although *myrkr*, a dark and muddy hollow, is also a possibility.

There were lanes leading into the more distant fields and meadows, wide enough for the movement of livestock and carts. White's Lane, now leading off Slough Road, follows ancient field boundaries out to Northmead, while the present Green Lane and Holmlea Road gave access to the further parts of Marshfield long before any dwellings were built along them.

The land actually called 'a common' was uncultivated rough pasture or waste, and all manorial tenants had the right to graze a regulated number of animals there, linked to their rights within the common fields. For many of the poorest tenants, use of the common as pasture and a source of wood or turves for fuel could have made the difference between survival and starvation. In Datchet there were two significant areas of common land. Datchet Common itself stretched eastwards as a thin strip from the edge of the village centre, widening out in a funnel shape to the boundary with Horton. Another long thin strip ran south from it towards Southlea and parallel to the river. This strip was called the *Forty*, not from its acreage but from an Old English word meaning a peninsula of higher ground projecting into a marshy area. Exactly as its name suggests, the level of the Forty differs from the land to either side, and it may represent the course or bank of an ancient Thames channel, which once ran in many minor strands before settling into its present single course.

Not all farmland was open; small 'closes' of private land were clustered around the village centre as farmyards, meadows, orchards and gardens. The present school playing field was once part of the manorial Saffron Close, which extended from Old Council Offices to Green Lane. Its name suggests that the herb plant, saffron, was grown there in the 16th or 17th centuries. The outlying estates of Riding Court and Southlea also had enclosed lands nearby. It can be seen from the map that old enclosures line the northern edge of Datchet Common along the road to Horton which was the original main through-route.

Datchet's main area of woodland was detached from the main settlement, much further north in Fulmer. However, the field name 'Running Groves' between Sumpter-mead and the Upton border implies that it was once a wooded grove, perhaps used as 'pannage'

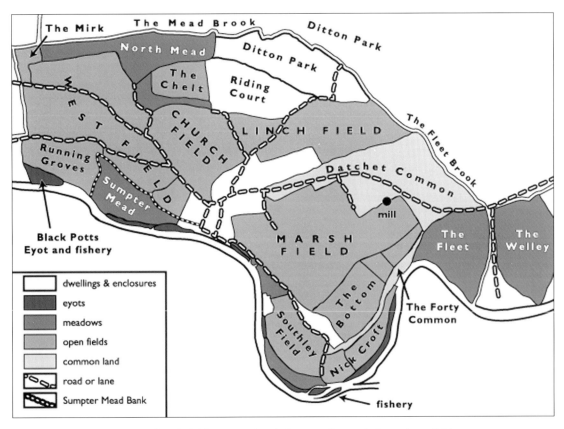

The Mirk

The Mead Brook

Ditton Park

North Mead

Ditton Park

The Chelt

Riding Court

WEST FIELD

CHURCH FIELD

LINCH FIELD

The Fleet Brook

Running Groves

Sumpter Mead

Datchet Common

mill

Black Potts Eyot and fishery

MARSH FIELD

The Fleet

The Welley

The Bottom

Nick Croft

The Forty Common

Southley Field

fishery

dwellings & enclosures
eyots
meadows
open fields
common land
road or lane
Sumpter Mead Bank

20 Medieval fields, extrapolated from enclosure information, 1834.

for the feeding of pigs. Willows would have been grown and cropped for many purposes along the riverside, and particularly on the many eyots or islands. These were prized possessions, mostly owned by the Lord of the Manor and Eton College. There was probably also scrubby woodland on the common.

In 1417 there is the first indication of a windmill serving Datchet, in a reference to *Milhouseacre* near the Fleet meadow. This is exactly the place still called Mill Lane, where the 18th-century miller's house survives.

The Lives of the People

In general, few written sources cast light on the lives of ordinary people before the 16th century, but there are several court cases in which events were recorded. In 1379 an inquest

was held into the death of John Bebegrave and the verdict was:

> John Bebegrave was mad. He was sitting at his midday meal at Datchet on Thursday 11th August and got up from it and ran to the Thames and jumped into the water, wilfully drowning himself. He had goods and chattels worth half a mark, for which Thomas Chanceaux is responsible.

In 1406 an inquiry was held to establish the age, and therefore the right to inherit, of John Arundel.[2] Such inquiries were necessary in the times before proper records of baptisms, which were not begun until the mid–16th century. John himself was of the nobility, but proof of his birth in 1385 was taken from more ordinary inhabitants who remembered, and could vouch for, the event.

Writ for proof of age of John, son of John Arundel junior, Knight, taken at Colnbrook, 12th August 1406. John Arundel, grandson and heir of Eleanor Arundel, was born at the Manor of Ditton on 1st August 1385 and baptised in St Mary's Church, Datchet, and he is therefore aged 21 years and more. Asked how they knew this, the jurors said:

William Spelyng, on that day went to the house of John Benet, vicar of Datchet, to ask him to be godfather.

Thomas Neel carried a torch at the baptism.

Henry Aleyn was a butler of Margery, then Lady Molyns, Lady of the Manor, and sent bread and wine for the baptism.

John Sperman on that day was sent to London by Lady Molyns to discover where the father could be found.

William Skynnere had a daughter born that day, who is now dead.

John Hale of Langley Marish had a new shop in Colnbrook on that day.

William Randolph had a daughter Joan married in St Mary's Church the following week to John Wellys.

Richard Auger was in church and held a cloth for the drying of hands after the baptism. John Fynton was a servant of Lady Molyns and carried two bottles of wine to the church for the people there to drink.

There are also several glimpses into criminal deeds from the past. In 1297 a pardon was issued, at the request of the Bishop of Lincoln, to Walter de Datchet for the death of Reynold son of Reynold Cost, and for any consequent outlawing. A similar pardon was granted in 1310 to Robert, son of Robert the Fisherman of Datchet, who was taken within the king's jurisdiction at Kennington, for the death of John le Ram of Datchet, as it appeared by the record of the steward and marshals of the King's household that he killed him in self defence. Another royal pardon was issued in 1439 to Nicholas Brown of Datchet who, on the previous day at Tewkesbury, 'with a knife worth 6d. held in the right hand, struck Philip Longe of Kaversham in the throat, whereof he died forthwith'. Robert the Fisherman, John le

Ram and Nicholas Brown are all known from other sources to have been significant landowners in Datchet.

There is written evidence for all these events, but the story most often told about medieval Datchet is folklore. It was first recorded in 1590 but embellished with more local detail by the time Ghyll told it in his 19th-century *History of Wraysbury*.[3] The story is set in the reign of Edward I (1272-1307), and concerns the bodies of 13 men who had been murdered at the *Ostrich Inn* in Colnbrook. They were being taken on a cart to be tipped into the Thames, when one body slipped off onto a strip of land by the Welley, near our Welley Road which is the boundary between the parishes of Datchet and Horton. A fisherman laying eel traps nearby is said to have suggested that the carters made the number of bodies up to 13 by throwing in one of themselves, but they retorted by shooting arrows intended to make him the 13th. The fisherman was not killed but walked into Colnbrook using an arrow as a stick and identified the gang, who were then caught. The story goes on to say that Horton refused to bury the body but Datchet parish did, thus claiming the strip of land for their parish. This has the ring of a real dispute about a parish boundary, and at a place where the boundary has actually changed. Curiously, the stretch of river near this point was called 'Colnbrook Churchyard' in the 18th and 19th centuries, and was where the victims of footpads were said to be thrown. There is one death or burial here for which there is real evidence; the top of a human skull was found with one of the Bronze-Age swords dug up in 1982 during gravel workings at the Welley, now Kingsmead Sailing Lake. When the skull was found it was assumed by some in the village to be proof of the 'Ostrich' story, but it remains uninvestigated and undated.

Chapter Three

The Royal Village:
16th and 17th Centuries

The Tudor and Stuart period was a high point in Datchet's history when it was a place of significance and some renown. This was almost wholly due to the ferry crossing over the Thames which was the most direct route for light traffic between Windsor Castle and the road to London. The ferry was under royal control as a perquisite of Datchet Manor until Charles I sold the Manor in 1630.

The Royal Courts and William Shakespeare

Royal use of the ferry is documented in the accounts of Kings Henry VII and VIII. Those for 1502 include several payments to 'the Ferryman at Datchet' for carrying Queen Elizabeth, wife of Henry VII, and her household over the Thames. Henry VIII's daughter, Princess Mary, had a household of her own as a very young child and was moved frequently between royal palaces. She spent a good deal of her time at Ditton Park which was conveniently near to Henry when he was at Windsor Castle. Among a number of accounts is one in 1517, when Mary was only a year old, 'for the passage over to Datchet ferry with my Lady Princess and her servants at two times, 3s. 4d.'. At Christmas in 1521, the princess was entertained by the clergy of Windsor College and Chapel, singing ballads and other songs before her. There also seem to have been mummers, as payment was made to 'John Thurgood, Lord of

Misrule, for divers garnitures and interludes exhibited before the Princess'. Other expenses for disguises and stage props include those 'To a man of Datchet for playing the friar before the princess'. Ditton Park was later given to Ann Boleyn, and though she received its revenues she did not actually live there.

In 1520, Henry VIII staged a fabulous Order of the Garter cavalcade from his palace at Richmond to Windsor Chapel for the Feast of St George.[1] The King, his Earls, Barons and Knights of the Garter, with all their horses, carriages and retinues, met the Queen's procession at Colnbrook:

> The Queen and the ladies and their companies stood in a field at the town's end beside the highway towards Windsor to see the King's noble company pass by, and then the Queen rode to the ferry next way to the Castle. The King rode by Slow [Slough] and so to Eton College, where all they of the College stood along, in manner of procession, receiving His Grace after their custom.

The 'next way' means the nearest way, Datchet ferry providing a direct and more private route for the court ladies from Colnbrook through Horton, along Datchet Common and down the High Street, see map 37. The approach over Windsor bridge through Eton provided a dramatic way for the king to arrive in procession at the castle, and the only route possible with a huge number of horses.

An engraving of the ferry boat in 1686 shows it to be flat, rather like a raft (or a barge, as it was described in the 13th century), able to carry several horses or a number of people. It could not have been used for heavy goods travelling by road which would have crossed by Windsor bridge. Just before 1700 the indefatigable traveller Celia Fiennes wrote in her journal on leaving Windsor Castle for London, 'Here I ferry over the Thames and so went a nearer way which is a private road made for the kings coaches, and so to Colebrooke'. The High Street was usually referred to as 'the King's Highway'.

William Shakespeare wrote *The Merry Wives of Windsor* for the 1597 feast of the Order of the Garter, though on this occasion the ceremony was held at Whitehall Palace in London. The play refers to places in and around Windsor which both Shakespeare and the Court knew well, including the fields called Datchet Meads, not actually in Datchet but on the castle side of the river. Near the present Victoria Bridge was the Hog Hole, a riverside ditch into which Falstaff was thrown after being carried out in a clothes basket through Datchet

Lane, still the approach to Windsor past the riverside station. One of the characters, called 'mine host of the Garter Inn' is identified as Richard Gallys, a wealthy burgess and three times mayor of Windsor. He is also known to have owned a house and land in Datchet in 1548, almost certainly the earliest parts of Goodwyn House in the High Street. Intriguingly, Datchet's parish registers show that families named Ford and Page lived in Datchet in the 1590s and it is tempting to suggest that 'Mistress Ford' and 'Mistress Page' in the play might also refer to people in Datchet known by Shakespeare.

Henry VIII granted the rights and profits of the ferry as a favour to members of his household, which he could do because he owned the manor and the ferry rights were part of its assets. In 1509 a grant was made to Christopher Rochester, groom of the chamber, and John Rookes, servant to the dean of the King's Chapel, 'to occupy, during pleasure, the ferry and ferry boat of Datchet'. In 1582, Queen Elizabeth leased the same rights to Maurice Hale, who was already her steward, managing the affairs of the manor and probably

21   Windsor Castle from Datchet ferry, 1686.

22 The first bridge, built 1706, drawn from the Datchet side by William Oram, published 1780. The house, far right, is on the old ferry land, the site of the present Datchet Lodge.

living at the Manor House in the village. The stretch of land facing the river, on which Datchet Lodge was built in the 18th century, had long been designated 'ferry land', with a cottage and other buildings for the running of the ferry business.

The riverfront is now, apart from the traffic, a peaceful place for sitting in the shade and feeding the ducks or fishing. But from medieval times until the middle of the last century this whole area, including the High Street, would have been a hub of activity serving trade and travel, see map 26. The river was a main route for both passengers and cargo and there was a wharf at Datchet, where the boat hire yard is now, for the loading and unloading of heavy goods brought by barge. A little way up the High Street there was a group of buildings called Coblers' Square, replaced by Park Villas in the 1850s. A cobler is a small flat boat, so that the square was very likely a boatyard, just a short haul up from the river's edge.

The centre section of the High Street occupies a slight rise in ground level which is sufficiently high to remain above flood level even under severe conditions. The Hat Hire Shop at number 20 is situated here and has the remains of a 15th- or early 16th-century timber-framed building at its core. It is known to have been called the *Rose* by 1612, a very common inn name at the time. Later its sign changed to the *Duke of Northumberland's Head* and it remained an alehouse until the 1740s when it became a butcher's shop. At various times during this period several other inns or alehouses are known to have existed along this short street, where the ferry and river traffic would have brought thirsty travellers and boatmen. At the top of the street there was an inn on each corner, of which one, the *Manor Hotel*, has survived in continuous use. It dates from the 16th century and has, until recent times, been directly owned and let by the Lord of the Manor. The earliest name recorded for it is the *Half Moon*, followed

23 The second bridge, built 1770, seen from the Windsor side, by Paul Sandby. Far left is Datchet Lodge, then Post House and Old Bridge House before the façades were remodelled.

24 The second bridge, built 1770, seen from the Windsor side, published by Tombleson. Old Bridge House has been remodelled since the Sandby drawing.

by the *Horse and Groom*. On the opposite corner was an alehouse which had a pin ball alley behind it. It was called *Piper's* in the 16th century and afterwards the *White Hart*.

Until the arrival of the railway and the removal of Datchet Bridge from the end of the High Street, there was no road from the riverside to Windsor. On reaching the west corner of the riverfront, a lane led round behind the High Street houses to rejoin the village centre. This is a typical medieval pattern of settlement; the dwelling plots facing the main street being long and thin with a back lane developing behind them as a connecting path. Back Lane was renamed Queen's Road in the late 19th century, in honour of Queen Victoria who used it in preference to the High Street on her way from Windsor. The roadway which now runs from the top of the High Street, in front of the *Morning Star* and round to Queen's Road, was called Hart's Lane from the *White Hart* inn on the corner.

The Thames at Datchet had always supported commercial fisheries, but Charles II and the great angler Isaak Walton fished here as a sport and pastime. Their favourite spot was the eyot called Black Potts, now crossed by the railway on the northern boundary of the parish. There was a fishing lodge here, built by Sir Henry Wotton, provost of Eton, which

was later used as a summer house by the painter Anthony Verrio who worked on redecorating the castle for Charles II. Alexander Pope described Charles returning from a fishing trip:

> Me thinks I see our mighty Monarch stand,
> The pliant rod now trembling in his hand;
> And see, he now doth up from Datchet come,
> Laden with spoils of slaughtered gudgeon home.

Horse racing was another of Charles II's sporting pastimes. From the 1670s the Datchet Ferry Plate race, a royal occasion, was run at Datchet Meads on the Windsor side. Francis Barlow's drawing of the scene at the last race attended by the King in 1687 includes the poetic quote:

> And Dorsett ever celibrated be,
> For this last honour which ariv'd to thee
> Blest for thy Prospect, all august, and gay,
> Blest for the memory of this glorious day.
> The last great Race the Royal Hero view'd
> O Dorsett to thy much lov'd plains he owed.'

However, in the 1690s there was also racing in Datchet itself, on the Common, advertised nationally for a valuable plate prize until Datchet was abandoned as a venue in favour of Ascot. It is often said that Charles II kept his mistress Nell Gwynne at Old Bridge House in Datchet since the queen refused to have her

25 Butcher's shop (now the hat shop), 20 High Street, taken in the 1970s before the remodelling of the shop front was remodelled. Externally an 18th- and 19th-century brick building, it has the timber-framed 'Rose' at its core.

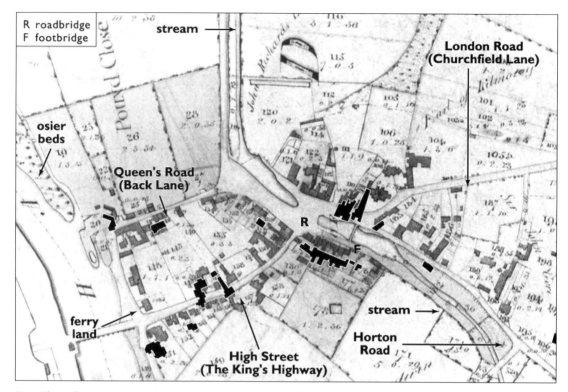

26 The village centre showing the watercourse and bridges, a detail from the enclosure map, 1834. Dark shading indicates those houses so far known or believed to survive at least in part from the 16th or 17th centuries.

living in the same county as herself. Datchet is the first place over the county boundary of the river, and Old Bridge House was the first suitable house reached after crossing by ferry, but the source of the story is not known and as yet there is no evidence to substantiate it.

The Lords of the Manor and Riding Court

The 16th century was generally a period of stability and confidence, with new business and professional classes emerging to modify the social hierarchy of medieval times. London developed enormously as the commercial and cultural capital, and Datchet was near enough to function as a country base for the newly rich. Windsor continued to be one of the chief royal palaces, with nearby Datchet attracting courtiers and officials as residents.

Riding Court was the grandest house in Datchet during the Tudor and Stuart period. From 1472 it had been the administrative base of the Manor of Datchet with Riding, but during the next century it emerged as an estate in its own right, leased from the crown by rich and powerful citizens. In 1544 Henry VIII granted the lease of Riding Court to Sir Maurice Berkeley, one of his gentlemen ushers of the Privy Chamber. The earliest memorial in the chancel of the church, a brass tablet with heraldic arms, records the death of Sir Maurice's wife, Katheryn, on 23 February 1559. Although the inscription does not mention it, she must have died in childbirth as their daughter Ann was baptised on 27 February in the same year. After Maurice's death in 1581 the estate was willed to his second son, as Riding was not the main family seat but a convenient base for London and Windsor.

In 1586, Richard Hanbury leased Riding Court from Queen Elizabeth I. He was a goldsmith, a citizen of London and thus a high status tenant. In 1604, during his tenancy, a survey of the manor described Riding Court in most unusual terms as 'a big farm', and as 'a large and beautiful dwelling house'. This comment on the grandeur of the house implies that he had some influence with the royal surveyors and was determined that his possession should be properly recognised. It is possible that Richard Hanbury rebuilt Riding Court and that it was still new and noteworthy in 1604. Very little of the present house now dates from before about 1800, though there was 17th-century panelling re-used in several rooms until 1930.

There is a brass memorial in the chancel of the church to Richard Hanbury's wife, Alice, who died in 1593. Gaps were left in the inscription to carry the details of Richard's death as well, but these were not added when he died in 1608. The plaque portrays Richard and his wife kneeling at an altar with their two daughters behind her and the arms of the City of London

27   Memorial brass to Katheryn Barkeley (Berkeley), 1559, St Mary's Church.

28   Memorial brass to Ales (d.1593) and Richard Hanbery (Hanbury) at St Mary's Church.

above, as Richard was a citizen there. The inscription is of interest as it throws light on the role of daughters at this time in a wealthy family with great social aspirations. One is recorded as having married Sir William Combe and the other Sir Edmond Wheeler, a London goldsmith like her father. Yet the names of these daughters were not given; in the absence of sons, their chief purpose was to create alliances through marriage to families with shared interests and to consolidate the father's status and wealth.

They were, of course, expected to produce sons to inherit the estates. It is known from other sources that the Hanbury girls were named Alice, who married William Combe and lived the rest of her life elsewhere, and Elizabeth, who became the wife of Edmond Wheeler and remained in Datchet. Elizabeth's first son, Richard, did not survive, but the second, born in 1601, was named Hanbury Wheeler, being given his grandfather's name to demonstrate his lineage. Hanbury Wheeler himself died at 32 with-

out heirs and the family's continued existence depended on his younger brother William. Unfortunately, William Wheeler had seven daughters and just one son, another William, who did not survive long enough to produce an heir. Ann, the eldest of the seven daughters, married Charles Pitcairne and they were styled Pitcairne alias Wheeler, a common device at the time to keep the name alive.

The unhappy fortunes of this family can be followed through memorials in the church. Hanbury Wheeler's death in 1633 is commemorated by a marble bust with an inscription on the chancel wall. The two other busts are memorials to John, Hanbury Wheeler's youngest brother who died in 1636, and to his sister Mary. She married Abraham Delaune and died in 1626 with her first son, Gideon. The brother who survived, William Wheeler, is commemorated by a grave slab in the chancel floor dated 1649. The last of this family group is an inscribed marble wall plaque to the

29 Memorial bust of Mary Delaune (neé Wheeler), d.1626, St Mary's Church.

30 Memorial bust of Hanbury Wheeler, d.1633, St Mary's Church.

31 Memorial bust of John Wheeler, d.1636, St Mary's Church.

memory of Katherine, the youngest of William Wheeler's daughters, who married John Balch, a London silk merchant, and died in 1679. It has been suggested that the busts of John and Hanbury Wheeler, and certainly several of the grave slabs, are by Edward Marshall, a sculptor of national standing whose London workshop was next door to the Wheeler's goldsmith's and banking premises in Fleet Street. The earliest of the three memorials, to Mary Delaune, is unusually classical in style for its date and is likely to be the work of a French artist, possibly Isaac Besnier.[2]

In 1631, Charles I sold the Manor of Datchet with Datchet St Helen's to Sir Charles Harbord, surveyor to the king, who almost immediately sold it to William Wheeler. On his memorial slab, Sir William Wheeler is described as the Lord of Datchet Manor, and in his will of 1649 Datchet was left to his only son William, who was then a child and died before maturity. In 1678 the seven daughters

of Sir William made claim to the Manor of Datchet, and it was won by the eldest, Ann Pitcairne alias Wheeler, whose son sold it to Budd Wase in 1680.

The Wase family held high office under Charles I and Charles II. William Wase, whose daughter Anne was married to Thomas Brinley, was one of the Auditors of the Revenue to both Charles I and II. Richard Budd was another of the King's Auditors and his wife Rose was Richard Hanbury's niece. A further intermarriage, and the passing on of a significant surname, must account for Budd Wase's curious name. Several more chancel grave slabs record the deaths of these families, who were related to each other in complex ways. When Budd Wase bought the Manor of Datchet in 1680, he had already been living at Riding Court for some time. His wife, Sarah, became Lady of the Manor after Budd's death until her own in 1712. She gave a beautiful silver flagon and plate to the church which are still in use today.

The Barker Family and Southlea

Robert Barker is one of Datchet's most colourful characters, and one who has left a lasting legacy both locally and nationally. His father Christopher was a printer, one of the enterprising newly rich moving into a country estate but with his business remaining at St Paul's Churchyard in London. Printing was a fast growing craft, the vehicle through which so many new religious and political ideas were disseminated. Christopher's eldest son, Robert, was born at his father's house at Southlea, which has not survived but was probably near the present farm and the 18th-century 'monastery' walls. (It is possible that parts of the old farm-house, demolished in recent years, may have been the Barkers' house.)

Christopher Barker was a London book-seller from 1569 and was printing books himself by 1575. He became styled Printer to the Queen because he had bought the patent, which we would now call a monopoly, to print all royal statutes and proclamations as well as all English bibles and books of Common Prayer. Christopher died at Datchet in 1599 and Robert took over all his father's patents for the duration of his life, and afterwards for his own sons, including the title of Printer to the Queen. In 1603, these patents were extended to include all books in Latin, Greek and Hebrew, and all charts and maps. This licence was bought in conjunction with Bonham Norton, the Barkers' business partner and the father-in-law of Robert's son, another Christopher. The marriage of Barker's son and Norton's daughter would not have been a coincidental love match, but a deliberate arrangement between the families to amalgamate and consolidate their interests. Robert is known to have taken as printing apprentices the sons of several yeoman–status families from Datchet, which would have indebted village society towards him as their patron.

The high point of Robert Barker's career and his greatest achievement was the beautiful printing in 1611 of the King James Authorised Bible from the new translation made at the Hampton Court Conference in 1604. The manuscript was bought by Barker for £3,500 and its printing was privately funded by Barker and Norton.

In his private affairs as much as in his business, Robert Barker was larger than life. By his first wife, Rachell, he had 12 children, all except one of whom survived. After Rachell's death in 1607 he married again and produced eight more. He erected a tomb memorial, now reduced to a wall plaque in the chancel of the church, to his father and his first wife, describing his father's work as finding printing rough as stone and leaving it smooth as marble. Appropriately, the memorial is not made of brass but of black marble. The inscription only occupies one half of the plaque, the other being left empty for his memorial to be added on his death, but it was never completed.

Christopher and Robert's business acumen is also seen in their accumulation of property in and around Datchet. In 1605 Robert bought the lease of Upton Manor, together with the medieval Upton Court house on the Datchet border, and in 1611 acquired the lease of the Eton College lands in Datchet. Most extraordinarily, in 1608 he paid the huge sum of £500 in order to obtain the lease of the rectory properties from St George's Chapel, which had already been promised to someone else, as well as £700 which was owing from the previous lease. The rectory was a great prize, as it made a considerable profit as well as conferring power locally. Such impressive financial dealing leads to the suspicion that Robert was not only extremely rich but also a megalomaniac, and he eventually overreached himself.

Bonham Norton had proved a troublesome, though very rich, partner. Robert must have been in financial difficulties by 1620, as his Datchet properties, including the Southlea estate, were then mortgaged to Bonham Norton. The office of Printer to King James I was also sold to him after bitter disputes, only to be bought back again by Robert Barker after Norton's death. The partnership between Barker and Norton had broken down and Robert was working with a different partner, Martin Lucas, in 1631. This was an extremely bad year for Robert Barker. Not only did his second wife die, but he became desperate to stop the import of books from abroad which threatened his monopoly. With Martin Lucas, he obtained a warrant to search for illegal imports, and went to Bristol where they had 60 incoming bibles seized. Even worse, the standards of his actual printing had fallen seriously, probably due to taking on far more work than could be properly supervised. Errors became frequent, and the most glaring caused his downfall. In the same year, 1631, he published a bible in which the word 'not' was omitted from the seventh commandment, which thus read, 'Thou shalt commit adultery'. It is tempting to speculate as to whether such a gross error was due to deliberate sabotage rather than negligence. As a result, Charles I's Star Chamber fined Barker and Lucas £3,000, ordering all copies to be returned for destruction, which is why 'The Wicked Bible' is a great rarity today. The fines were not paid by 1635 when Robert was committed to debtor's prison, and they were probably still not paid at the time of his death there in 1645.

Datchet itself has benefited from Robert Barker's sad end. In 1644 he was clearly sorting out his affairs as far as possible and he established a trust in Chancery for the management of the Bridge House charity, see pages 36 and 54. Barker's name was also remembered by the London printers, for in 1651 they complained about the monopoly of the right to print bibles, by then in the hands of Robert's son, Matthew. In 1660 they went further in their complaints, claiming that the Barker family had hidden the manuscript so that no other printer could work from it. Whether this was true or not, the licence to print bibles remained in the family's possession until 1709. It is surprising that Robert, having produced a total of 19 surviving children, did not found a dynasty in Datchet. His eldest son, Christopher, and two of his daughters are known to have continued in occupation of the Rectory House for some time, but within a generation all trace of the family had gone from Datchet. Although the monument he left in the church for his own death to be recorded was never completed, a memorial tablet has been erected by the Barker Bridge Trust and beneath it is displayed a small bible printed by Robert Barker in 1614 which the church recently bought.

32 Title page of a Bible printed by Robert Barker, 1614.

Christopher and Robert Barker's grandiose ambitions had a lasting effect on land ownership in Datchet. From 1570 Christopher deliberately appears to have set about extending his property centred on Southlea. He bought up all available land, including several substantial freehold estates, and a number of houses within the village. Robert continued to buy land after his father's death in 1599, quite apart from owning the leases of Upton Court, the rectory and Eton College estates. Two fisheries, probably those mentioned in Domesday Book, were also in Barker hands. One was to the south of Datchet near Southlea, leased from Eton College, and the other is probably represented by the house called the Willows at the corner of the riverside, leased from Datchet Manor. (This was still a fishery run by the Newman family throughout the 18th and 19th centuries.)

By the 1620s Robert Barker's possessions were valued as the next highest after Riding Court itself. To a similar value were the estates of Bernard, John and Maurice Hale, and all of these owners' holdings far exceeded the property of any other landowners. (This was the same Hale family, present in Datchet from before 1400, who held the ferry rights and the stewardship of the Manor in the reign of Elizabeth.)

Aggrandisement of large estates at the expense of smaller ones has been shown to be a feature of the late 16th century in many other places, even though the land so held continued to be managed within the common field system. The Hale properties were divided by inheritance within the next century, but the Barker estate remained intact. This was due to its being mortgaged to Robert's partner and son-in-law, Bonham Norton, and then sold on or bequeathed as a single estate. It is still identifiable in the 18th century when Edward Lascelles inherited both the Datchet and Upton Court estates. By the time of enclosure in 1810 the Lascelles family were awarded a share of the available land equal to that of the Lord of the Manor; an impact almost entirely attributable to Christopher and Robert Barker's purchasing power.

Farming in the Common Fields

The common fields survived in Datchet right up to 1810 when enclosure took place, although it is certain that more closes of land came into private ownership during the intervening centuries. Unfortunately there is no map to show how the land was organised, whether individual holdings were gradually amassed together or remained widely scattered. One source suggests that the land parcels remained remarkably stable; Eton College's lands were surveyed in detail in 1597, each plot being described in terms of all the adjacent owners. When this was copied in the 1790s and the current owners' names inserted, the plot descriptions remained otherwise exactly the same. From the 1680s the manor courts recorded frequent encroachments (enclosing by fencing or building) made upon common land or near dwelling houses, a move toward the consolidation of private land. While such encroachments were officially required to be thrown open again, owners may have been allowed to come to an arrangement with the Lord to retain what they had taken.

The organisation of farming must have been under manorial control from medieval times, but, although the manor court rolls survive from 1565, the first written agricultural orders date from the Court of 1630. These deal with the control of livestock on the common and in the fields after harvest, listing fines due for unringed hogs, cattle not branded with a D, and for the keeping of sheep above the stint. 'Stinting' was restricting the number of animals each owner was entitled to keep on the common fields, according to his land holding and the common rights it conferred. It was regulated in varying ways right up to enclosure. In 1633 the orders enlarged upon this by stating that every ancient cottager (i.e. cottager having customary rights from beyond legal memory), 'shall common for a cow, a bullock, a hog and a pig and no more'. This indicates that the common fields, as well the actual common, were coming under some pressure from over use, confirmed by another enactment at the same court. Five wealthy inhabitants were presented to be 'at fault for having newly erected cottages without four acres of land being attached to each of them'. This amount of land was stipulated by a Parliamentary Act of 1589, although it is doubtful whether it was ever enforceable.

The 'jury' of the manor court, which made and enforced these decisions, consisted of 12 of the chief farming tenants presided over by the Lord's steward, while all tenants and owners were in theory supposed to attend the Court. The jurors also chose manorial officials from among their number, known as the headboroughs and haywards. The headboroughs were responsible for a very wide range of local law-enforcing and tax-collecting duties, while the haywards, or field drivers, supervised the upkeep of fences and control of animals in the common fields. The manor court also played a role in what was chiefly the parish church business of beating the bounds at Rogationtide in May. This custom, revived in recent times for entertainment, was necessary in an age before there were maps to determine whether or not the parish's land had been encroached upon. All significant boundary points were marked by a stone, an identifiable tree or a stake which could be recognised on the next occasion. The first of recurring references to this 'bound staking day' is in 1634, when 12 May was fixed for all men to meet at Bells Elm (presumably near the *Five Bells* inn, now the *Royal Stag*), by eight o'clock in the morning, 'to go a staking' upon payment of a fine for absence. A different custom was first recorded on 27 October 1646, when all the jury of the manor court were to meet at the bridge foot 'for staking of the fields'. This was the marking out, literally with 'landmarks', of individual plots and access routes in the common arable fields and meadows since the plots were not fenced around. Staking took place during the autumn before ploughing began and was irregularly recorded right

through to the end of the 18th century. In 1698 there was an order for the jury also to set out the ancient meereways (boundaries) and banks in the common fields, 'as near as may be', implying that these divisions between territories had been encroached upon.

In the 1640s other matters for which fines were payable began to be recorded; the breaking of other men's hedges or lopping of their trees, fences left down, ditches not being scoured and land banks not properly made up. This last was of extreme importance in a place so liable to flood. On urgent occasions all landholders were required to send their teams of horses or oxen, or a man to work for as long as needed. The whole length of the river bank had to be maintained, as well as the flood banks further inland, particularly Sumptermead bank (see map 20), which is still a feature of the golf course. Owners and tenants were responsible for the regular repair of sections of fences, river banks and flood banks adjacent to their own land, and the courts fined those who did not comply. Everyone suffered for the failure of individuals in a communal system, and the most wealthy owners were as likely to be penalised as the humblest tenant.

The Village Centre and Road Routes
(See map 26 for this whole section)
From the Thames ferry the King's Highway, now the High Street, led up to the village centre where another waterway had to be crossed. Until the mid-19th century, Datchet was not a village around a green, but a village around a long thin marshy pond, sometimes called a 'hollow way'. It was fed by a stream from the Slough border (probably a paleo-channel of the ancient Thames), which ran out through the village as Linchfield Brook and emptied into the river near Wraysbury. Where it widened to lie as a pool it was called Pillers or Pillards Pool, an intriguing name for which there are several possible explanations. The first is that the village stocks or pillory was nearby, in front of the Manor House, where summary

justice would have been dispensed. Another is that the Old English word 'pyll', meaning pool, may have survived until it was understood to be the actual name of that specific pool and the general word 'pool' was added to it. 'Piller' can also mean 'robber', which leads to interesting speculations. The stream would have provided a water supply and there is still a memory in the village of a great grandmother fetching water from it for washing laundry, an oral tradition from before the 1840s when it was culverted underground.

There was a road bridge crossing the pool from the top of the High Street to a point near the present chemist's shop. The first known reference to it is in the court roll for 1565, recording the inheritance of a house 'lying at the end of Pillers Bridge on the south part of the bridge'. (This house later became the *White Hart*, on the corner site of the modern off-licence.) In 1570 Queen Elizabeth I, who owned the Manor and used the bridge, gave a cottage and land to the inhabitants of the village, the rent of which was to provide for 'the repair of Datchet Bridge'. The cottage and land, de-scribed as 'Churchlands', was the old part of the present *Royal Stag* adjoining the church-yard. Manorial surveys of 1604 and 1622 show that it was in the hands of a group of prominent inhabitants of the village for the upkeep of the bridge, but no formal Trust was as yet established. Then in 1644 the ubiquitous Robert Barker, as the last survivor of those in charge, caused events to take a different turn. While imprisoned as a debtor, and shortly before his death, he established a new Trust which came to bear his name. The deed assigned the house and lands, 'commonly known as the Bridge House', to 17 inhabitants, including William Wheeler, William Wase and George Vaux, but did not state the purposes for which the property was to be used, nor did it refer to the bridge. This was the origin of 'Robert Barker's Bridge House Trust', which still benefits the village today, but the property was first designated by Queen Elizabeth and

was already known as the Bridge House before Robert Barker's 1644 deed.

Just to the west of the Bridge House was a cottage on the site of the parish drop-in centre, confusingly now called 'The Bridge'. In 1548 this building was recorded as being under the control of the overseers of the poor, two inhabitants appointed as unpaid parish officers. Every parish was required to raise a rate from householders to support their own poor, old or infirm people. Severe laws were passed to ensure that paupers remained in, or were returned to, their own parish, to allay the very real fears of roving beggarly people, and this cottage was a poorhouse or almshouse used to house Datchet's own paupers. Next to the almshouse was the Rectory House with its yards and barns, and then Eton College's barn on the Bank House site. Thus most of the prop-erty on the north side of the village was owned by the church and collegiate institutions, and had been so from medieval times.

On the opposite side the whole of the present Manor House range of buildings belonged to the Lord of the Manor and were rented directly from him, as they continued to be until the early years of the present century. Riding Court was the administrative base for Datchet Manor from 1472, but there was also a significant house here by the 16th century, although it is unlikely to have been lived in by the Lord of the Manor. In the survey of 1604 it was described as a mansion house and was occupied by Maurice Hale, who was probably the steward of the manor and also owned the ferry rights. After the Manor of Datchet was separated from Riding Court and sold in 1630, it is more likely that the manor courts were held here in the village. It is not until the 18th century that there is written evidence for the main building being called the Manor House, as it still is today.

A photograph taken in the 1960s during work on the church steeple clearly shows the difference between the north and south sides of the village centre, now separated by the

33 Looking south from the church steeple, 1964. In the foreground is the *Royal Stag*, almshouse and Rectory House; opposite is the Manor House range, including Old Council Offices on the left.

Greens, but in the past by the pool running through. On the north, the medieval buildings and sites are clustered closely in the foreground around the church. To the south, the whole Manor House range, from the present site of the school along to the *Manor Hotel* corner and the top of the High Street, curves gently along what was the edge of the pool.

The Manor House itself is a substantial and high status late 16th-century house, and its building or rebuilding may coincide with Maurice Hale's occupation. In the mid-17th century a new wing was added to the house at its eastern end, with higher rooms and a taller gable, which is still evident in the present roof line and internal floor levels. An addition at this date could be connected with the sale of the Manor and a new role for the Manor House. Although the whole building is now disguised by an 1870s mock Jacobean façade, much of the original timber frame remains

34 Drawing of the Manor House before the remodelling, published in 1858. From Tighe and Davis, *Annals of Windsor*, 1858.

visible inside and its earlier appearance is known from a drawing done before the remodelling. The front is shown as plastered over, which was a common alternative to having the timbers exposed and is also seen at Church Cottage.

Other buildings along this range would have been associated with the main house; in 1604 there were two barns, stables, outbuildings, an orchard, garden and yard. Adjacent to the main house on the west are Manor Cottage and Manor Green Cottage, which were originally one house and contemporary with the late 16th-century Manor House. Their fashionable 18th-century brick façades conceal the most unexpected exposed timber frames inside. Next along is the *Manor Hotel* which, although much extended, has a 16th-century building at its core. Between two modern blocks to the east of the main house the tiny Old Council Offices has survived, possibly from the earliest phase of building on the site. It has also acquired a mock timbered façade, related to the work done at the Manor House and disguising its original timber-framed construction.

From the village centre the main route to London is now along London Road, but until the 18th century this road only led to Riding Court and Ditton. In 1660 it was called Churchfield Lane and, apart from Church Cottage on the corner and a house on the site of the present Datchet House, there was no other development along its route. Traffic for London would have used the road to Horton and on to Colnbrook, an important travelling stage out of London. Very early development occurred along the north side of Horton Road, because this was the main axis out of the village centre and on the fringe of Datchet Common, see map 47. By the 16th century this was becoming as built up as the village centre, a complex of plots and houses being bought, built and extended by the wealthy alongside the hovels of the poor. Eton College owned land here, as did St George's Chapel. At the opposite end of the village, there was no expansion westwards at all, probably due to the marshy nature of the land and the stream entering Datchet alongside the lane to Upton and Eton.

The Reformation and the Church

In 1536 Henry VIII began the dissolution of the monasteries, following his decision to renounce papal supremacy and become head of the Church of England himself. The chantry chapel at Ditton was also dissolved, in about 1547. The property belonging to the Priory of St Helen's in Bishopsgate was seized and sold, which had repercussions for Datchet because the Manor of St Helen's was absorbed into the Manor of Datchet and its land released for sale. The Barker family's estate at Southlea almost certainly originated as part of the Priory's farm, and had already been sold at least once before Christopher Barker bought it in 1583. Henry's injunction, in 1538, that every parish should purchase a Bible helped create an expanding market for printers, and one for which the Barker family eventually owned the monopoly.

The people of Datchet would have been very aware of alarming events in Windsor in 1544, when Robert Testwood, Anthony Pierson and Henry Filmer, the 'Windsor Martyrs', were found guilty of heresy as Lutheran sympathisers. (While Henry VIII renounced the supremacy of the Pope, he did not endorse the more radical views of Calvin and Luther.) The jury which convicted them was composed of tenants of the dean and canons of St George's, which almost certainly included the rector of Datchet and perhaps his under-tenants. They were burnt at the stake near the present George V monument on the road from Windsor to Datchet, and shouted to the people watching to 'stand fast in the truth of the Gospel'. All were local clergy, as was Robert Marbeck who was tried with them but pardoned. He was organist to St George's Chapel and a key figure in the Reformation struggles.

The vicar of Datchet, who may well have been in the crowd watching the martyrs burn, was Hugh Gifford, appointed in 1522 long before the religious crises arose. He remained in post throughout Henry VIII's and Edward VI's reigns, but his term ended in 1553. This was the year of the catholic Queen

Mary's accession, and so he may by then have too protestant in his views to continue as vicar. Gifford would already have complied with changes to old rituals and demands to remove images, votive candles and decorations. He would have been required to use the new Book of Common Prayer, and read official sermons from the *Book of Homilies* at least four times a year. Protestantism laid stress on the need to bring the Gospels to the people, and on regular preaching which many poorly educated clergy were unqualified to do. The fact that St George's bought, for 20d., a *Book of Homilies* for Master Gifford in 1548 implies that he was not considered a competent preacher in his own right. In 1552, near the end of Edward VI's reign, he would also have seen the making of an inventory of the church's valuable possessions, with a view to confiscation. Of the seven chalices and crosses listed, as well as six holy pots and candle-sticks, eight great bells and two small ones, nothing has survived. Richard Koos was the next vicar, during Mary's reign when catholic ritual was reimposed. It was at this time that the chancel of the church in Datchet was reported to be ruinous, due to the fault of the dean and canons of St George's, though such a state was fairly common throughout the country. In 1559 Datchet again had a new vicar, and as this was the year following the accession of Elizabeth, it may be assumed that the return to protestantism was the cause for another change of clergyman.

Throughout the 17th century the parlous state of the building and its furnishings was complained of in bishops' visitations, although wealthy families, including the lords of the manor, erected grand monuments to themselves there. Minor canons of St George's Chapel, from whom the vicars were chosen, several times took Datchet 'on account of the poorness of its living', implying that they had other sources of income from elsewhere. Even worse, three vicars between the 1630s and 1680s seem to have been a positive danger to the spiritual life of the parish. Edward Stamp was suspended from the privileges of the Chapel due to allegations of lax morals. The case was investigated, his name was cleared and he was reinstated. Then John Davis was said to have 'Failed of doing his duty at the parish of Datchet where he has been a person of light and scandalous behaviour'. He was also accused of Roman Catholic tendencies and was dismissed from both the living of Datchet and the Chapel. He was followed by John Maidstone whose behaviour was no better; 'He had come drunk to church, he openly had a scandalous frequentation with another man's wife, and has had a woman suspected of being a lewd woman in his house'. A strange situation occurred in the years 1677 to 1682, when the number of marriages recorded in the parish register soared from one or two a year to over twenty, while none were conducted at St George's Chapel in the same period. This might prove to be a case of a 'marriage shop' where the vicar was prepared to marry couples clandestinely, without banns or licence, and far from their own parish. The other explanation, that Datchet's church was an alternative to St George's, seems unlikely, and further research is needed to clarify what was going on.

In 1669, the Bishop of Lincoln conducted an inquiry into the activities of nonconformists (their assemblies being called conventicles), as they were liable to heavy fines. Anthony Taylor, the vicar of Datchet, replied that, 'There is not any conventicle kept, the people are uniform and obedient to commands'. The people may well have been obedient in Datchet itself, but they did not have to go far if they wanted to practise alternative beliefs. In Horton at the same time there were groups of Quakers and Antipaedobaptists, including two 'inveterate' Baptist teachers who had been excommunicated from the Church of England. Colnbrook was a positive hotbed of nonconformity; several hundred people came from Windsor, Staines and other places to the Presbyterian Chapel and to a Quaker house. The fact that Colnbrook was a market town on a main route goes some way to explaining this, as several of the ministers are described as living in London. A Dissenters' Meeting House in Datchet was registered at the dwelling of Robert Greenhough in 1698, but there is no further reference to this and nonconformity was not established here until near the end of the next century. The other main group outside the Church of England, the Roman Catholics, had to be reported at the Quarter Sessions Courts. Richard and Edward Cole, who lived in the predecessor of Datchet House, were fined in the 1680s and '90s as 'popish recusants' alongside Henry Palmer of Dorney Court.

The Lives and Deaths of the People

The records of the Quarter Sessions Courts at Aylesbury provide some glimpses into life in Datchet towards the end of this period, although there is no surviving evidence of serious crimes being committed. The alehouses were a constant source of trouble, both for being unlicensed and for allowing unruly behaviour. In the 1680s, Henry Newman was fined three times for keeping unlicensed alehouses, as was Josiah Beesouth in the 1690s. Richard Smith was taken to court for assaulting Henry Newman in 1688, and Henry himself was then twice bound over to keep the peace. (The Newman family was first recorded here in 1605 and may have been the same family line which finally died out in the 1930s with the Misses Newman of Holiman's Plat in the High Street.) Another related Henry Newman, a baker, ill-treated his apprentice, James Lawrence, so badly that the court released James from his apprenticeship and ordered Henry to return half the premium paid to him as the master. Newman had 'very grossly abused his apprentice by unmercifully beating him, notwithstanding that James Lawrence served him as was his duty'.

Very little is known about the poor in Datchet because the parish records dealing with them have not survived. However, registers of all baptisms, marriages and burials were ordered to be kept from 1538 and Datchet's series begins in 1559, the year after Elizabeth became Queen. These registers record some very sad deaths, as well as irregular births where the name of the father was significant for the future maintenance of the child. Henry Newman, a member of the troublesome family already mentioned, was 'the reputed father' of a child born to Alice West in 1600. In the 1680s John Wansel fathered two children upon his housekeeper, though it is noted that he did marry her later. An unnamed child was baptised in 1688, who had been born to 'a whore who was delivered of a daughter in the field called Running Groves', land which is now part of the golf course. Deaths as well as births occurred in the fields; in 1614, 'a poor man who died on Goodman Berrington's land' was buried, and in 1592 a poor woman died in Berrington's barn. Four years later, 'George, a poor boy, died in Richard Bavin's hay house'. Since these incidents were thought worthy of comment by the vicar or parish clerk at the time, they were probably very unusual. Only one death was reported to have been by drowning in the Thames, that of Roger, a servant to Mr. Bellamy in 1581, apart from six who drowned in a ferry accident in 1594 and were buried at Windsor.

In the register of burials, an outbreak of the plague is recorded, brought from London to Windsor and then to Datchet. The disease was endemic on a small scale both before and after the great outbreak in the 1660s. In 1603, an unnamed servant was buried; 'a gentleman's man lying at Thomas Tripp's house of this parish, the King's Majesty [James I] keeping court at Windsor, the said gentleman's servant died out at Mr. Tripp's house of the plague and was buried the 20th July'. The next entry is, 'Two children of the said Thomas Tripp, by name Andrew and Annis, were buried the 30th July', followed by, 'Thomas Tripp the father of the two children was buried the 13th August'. A man and his wife died of the plague in the summer of 1605, but no other outbreaks are recorded.

Deaths by suicide would not have been entered in the burial register as they would have been denied the rites of the church. There is a persistent story that the burial place for suicides was the triangle of grass at the point where Queen's Road meets Slough Road near the level crossing. The story, recorded by Samuel Osborn in his *History of Datchet* in 1887, was based on an oral tradition which could have reached back at least another hundred years. He also said that skeletons had been found there, but this has not yet been confirmed. It is certainly a likely place, being at a crossroads at the furthest end of the village from the church. If it is so, then one Robert Mathew may have been buried there in 1565, during the night, without a coffin, and with a stake through his body, as was the custom. The manor court rolls state that he killed himself, 'Not having the fear of God before his eyes but through the instigation of the devil, by throwing himself into the water of the fosse'. (The fosse was the ditch or brook bounding the parish to the west, north and east.) This was the standard wording for verdicts of self-killing, which became far more common from about 1530 than it had previously been. The cause for such an increase was partly the intense religious turmoil of the period, when the presence of the devil was felt to be a constant threat and was linked to beliefs in witchcraft. Another unpleasant reason for the rise in suicide verdicts was a Tudor Act of Parliament which required the deceased's goods to be forfeited to the Crown's agents, so that an element of greed might be involved in the coroner's verdict. In earlier times, when John Bebegrave drowned himself in the river in 1379, the more lenient verdict of madness was much more common and would have avoided a desecrated burial for the victim.

The Civil War and Restoration

Events in Datchet during this period were played out against the background of the Civil War from 1642 to 1649, followed by the rule of Cromwell, and then by the Restoration of the monarchy in 1660. The proximity of Windsor meant that Datchet was well aware of both the king's and parliament's activities. Charles had intended to make Windsor his headquarters and was reported to be raising troops there, but it was too near London and the town was not sympathetic. He left for York and the Parliamentary forces took control. Prince Rupert bombarded the castle from a base at Eton, but to no avail. From 1642 to 1648, Windsor became Sir Thomas Fairfax's training ground for Cromwell's New Model Army. Some 4,000 soldiers were billeted in the homes of the population of the town and neighbouring villages, or camped in the Castle park.

In 1647 Datchet was one of the villages 'in that part of the County of Bucks which is next adjoining Windsor Castle', whose inhabitants signed a petition of complaint to Parliament and Thomas Fairfax about the billeted troops, asking for compensation or relief. They declared that in some houses between twenty and forty soldiers had been quartered for long periods, the inhabitants having to provide for them, which added to the great burdens already imposed by the war. They claimed that many of them were deeply in debt, that they could not set their labourers to agricultural work as normally, that food was becoming scarce and prices high. Everyone was affected, freeholders, farmers and labourers, together with their wives and children. There are 29 signatures (or marks) on the Datchet petition, representing virtually all householders, and including that of William Wheeler the Lord of the Manor, William Wase, three members of the Hale family and George Vaux of Datchet House.

During the rule of Cromwell, the revenues of religious institutions, including St George's, were confiscated and put to secular

35 Petition to Parliament, complaining about billeted troops, 1647. Legible signatures include William Wheeler, George Vaux, John Hale, Bernard Hale senior & junior, Henry Newman, William Mathewe, John Styles.

uses such as paying the army, but from 1649 their lands began to be sold. In 1659, Datchet Rectory, along with others owned by St George's, was sold through a panel of trustees who were aldermen or citizens of London, one of whom was Thomas Arnold. The following year, when the monarchy was restored, these 'late pretended sales' were investigated and the lands restored to their previous owners. However, the Arnold family maintained a connection of some kind with Datchet as they leased the rectory from St George's in the early 1700s.

Most local people would have been unlikely to have actively supported the king or parliament during the Civil War; they were more concerned about the immediate impact of either army upon their lives. However, Sir Ralph Winwood and his son Richard, who owned Ditton Park from 1615, were more closely involved. Sir Ralph was Secretary of State under James I, but Richard supported the parliamentary cause, though as a moderate. While generally keeping in the background, he offered hospitality to Cromwell's associate Bulstrode Whitelock at Ditton Park, and provided falcons for Cromwell to hunt in Windsor Forest. The vicar at Datchet, John Batchelor, is known to have been ejected from his living in 1660, presumably for his puritan views, but he continued to preach privately to Mrs. Winwood in her chamber at Ditton Park in the years after the Restoration. He was apparently not preaching openly in the chapel there, which Richard Winwood had rebuilt and endowed. By 1680 Richard was re-elected to parliament, having managed with tact and diplomacy, or deliberate cunning, to offend neither side.

There is a curious political tract, written in 1681, in defence of the right to succession of Charles II's Roman Catholic brother, James, Duke of York. Charles had summoned parliament to meet at Oxford to avoid the interference of the strongly protestant City of London, and the tract takes the form of a dialogue about the implications of such a move. It purports to be between 'Sam, the ferryman at Datchet, Will, a waterman of London and Tom, a bargeman of Oxford'. Its obscure content is of little interest now, but it is highly significant that the fictional ferryman at Datchet is treated on a par with similar characters from Oxford and London. The implication is that Sam will be as recognisable to readers as Will and Tom, and is clear evidence for the national reputation of Datchet and its ferry at the time.

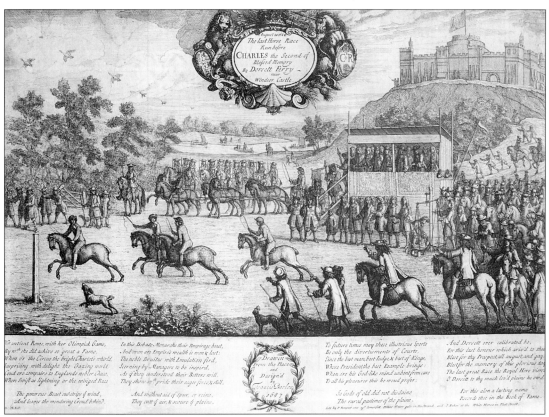

36 Charles II at Datchet ferry races, 1687, by Francis Barlow. The races took place at Datchet Meads, on the Windsor side of the river; the ferry may be suggested in the background.

Chapter Four

Thames Bridges and Troubled Times: 18th and Early 19th Centuries

In 1706, the ancient ferry was replaced by a bridge over the Thames from the foot of the High Street. It was rebuilt three times after that, the last bridge being demolished in 1851. Datchet is the only Thames bridge which has been lost, although it was replaced by two others, above and below the original site. During the course of the 18th century Datchet seems to have prospered increasingly, partly due to the presence of the bridge, but the end of this century and the beginning of the next was a period of decline and difficulties, due to both national and local causes.

The Four Thames Bridges

The Hale family had been operating the ferry for nearly 150 years, but now perhaps one 'Mr. Hale's' inefficiency contributed to its demise. The Royal household had found the ferry unsatisfactory for some time, as is evident from this message sent in 1678:

> From Secretary Coventry to Mr. Hale, Keeper of the ferry boat at Datchet Ferry. One of the Messengers, sent two days ago on His Majesty's service, has complained that he was forced to make a long stay before he could get you to give him passage. You cannot but know it is your duty, whenever any messenger or express rides on the King's service, to give immediate passage on demand, whether by night or day. Therefore, let me have no more of these complaints, for, if I have, you must hear from me in another manner.

Although Andrew Pitcairne-Wheeler sold the Manor of Datchet to Budd Wase in 1680, he seems to have kept for himself the ferry rights belonging to the Manor, as he mortgaged these rights for £1,000. In 1699 he wrote to King William III to complain that a wall built by His Majesty was threatening the running of the ferry and that the lender might call in the mortgage, which would ruin him. This wall, part of major improvements to the Castle grounds towards the river, ran alongside the river on the Windsor side. Outside it there was space for a road running along the river bank, with a narrow footpath leading through the wall directly to the Castle. The king bought the ferry rights from Wheeler for more than £7,000, and had trees felled in Windsor Forest to start the building of a bridge. After King William's death in 1702 no more work was done until 1706 when Queen Anne had the wooden bridge completed, according to the Lord Treasurer, 'for the better convenience of our passage from our Castle at Windsor'.

This route was frequently used by the Queen and her great favourites, the Duke of Marlborough and his wife Sarah, who occupied Langley Park for about ten years as it was nearer to London than Blenheim. A carriage drive-way, known as Marlborough Drive, was built from the house, past Langley church, crossing Ditton Park to Datchet and on over the bridge

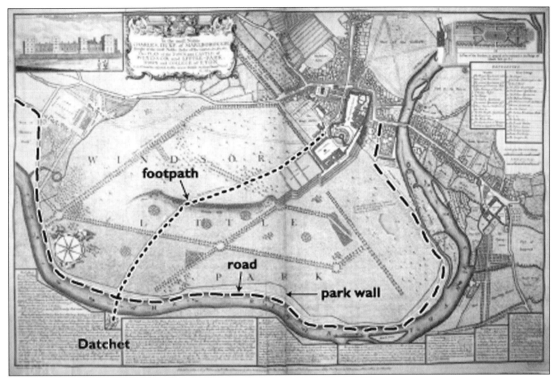

37 Routes over Datchet Bridge to Windsor, 1742.

to Windsor. Abigail Masham, who supplanted Sarah Marlborough as the queen's confidante, also lived at Langley and continued to use the drive, of which sections still exist, including Green Drive near Langley church.

The new Datchet Bridge was toll-free for all traffic, so it quickly became preferred to Windsor Bridge, causing the Windsor authorities a dramatic loss of tolls at their bridge.[1] These tolls had always been a considerable part of the income of the Corporation of the town, and while the Treasury did not see any reason why the queen should not make a bridge on her own land, especially where there was already a ferry, compensation was paid to the town. Maidenhead Corporation made a similar complaint, and, although it was not upheld, it does indicate how much traffic was choosing the new free route through Datchet. The only known representation of

the first Datchet Bridge is a drawing by the artist William Oram which was published in 1780, 10 years after the structure itself had been replaced. Oram lived at Sandlea House, a little further down the river at Southlea. The 1706 bridge can be distinguished from the later ones as it is built entirely of wood, while the all the others are supported on stone piers.

The first bridge was repaired in 1734, at a cost of £800, but it was completely rebuilt in 1770, again paid for by the Crown. This second bridge had a wooden deck resting on nine substantial stone piers, the remains of which have been found recently during river dredging. There are three different known prints of the second bridge, and two more showing the piers which remained after the superstructure collapsed during heavy floods in 1794. At that point King George III provided a free ferry service alongside the piers which

38   The second bridge, built in 1770, seen from the Datchet side, artist unknown.

39   Ruined piers of Datchet Bridge, *c.*1795, by J. Hakewill.

40   The reinstated ferry, *c.*1795, by William Havell. On the Windsor side is the *Crown and Angel* inn.

remained in mid-stream. A well known print by Havell shows this reinstated ferry being drawn across on a rope, carrying a small wagon and operating from a wooden jetty on the Datchet side, with the *Crown and Angel* public house on the Windsor bank.

While prepared to offer a ferry service, George III was adamant that the Crown was not going to pay for yet another new bridge, which he considered the responsibility of the county authorities. Both Berkshire and Buckinghamshire denied this, as the bridge had originally been provided by Queen Anne, and a long argument ensued. Eventually, in 1801, John Richards, the rector of Datchet, indicted both counties for failing to carry out their duty. Richards was a lawyer and a most contentious character in his own right, but on this occasion he was acting in the interests of all the local inhabitants. In 1809, after a King's Bench court case, both counties were directed to pay half the cost of rebuilding which came to a total of £2,375 each. The old piers were re-used, although there had been earlier proposals for an iron or a stone bridge. Part of the problem was that, as the bridge had originally been toll-free, permission for toll-charging to pay for a more ambitious construction was refused.

When the third bridge was opened in 1811 there was great revelry in Datchet, fuelled by the alcohol needed for a proper celebration, to which Queen Adelaide and wealthy inhabitants of the village contributed. Further excitement was provided by a 'pugilistic encounter' between a keeper of Windsor Great Park and George Gosden (who will be heard of again), after Gosden had ridden his horse across the bridge before the Queen herself passed over it. Gosden, then aged 65, gave the much younger keeper 'a good licking', and his blood, or 'claret', was reported to have flown freely. Such celebrations in the village show how vital the bridge was seen to be, both for ease of local travel and for the bringing of through trade. The role played by the village's own rector, in forcing the authorities to rebuild, must also have brought much local satisfaction.

Then by 1834 the superstructure was again unsafe, and this time even worse antagonism broke out. The two counties had agreed that their boundary should run through the centre of the bridge, and it was the Datchet

41 The third bridge, built 1811, from the Datchet side, by R.C. Buckler, 1822.

side that was in need of repair. Berkshire refused to contribute on the grounds that they were responsible only for their own half, and not for half of all repairs. At that point, Berkshire's own side was found to be about to collapse and the county suggested rebuilding in iron instead. Buckinghamshire refused, and then in 1836 their half fell down and a temporary ferry operated again. This time, each county started their own half from their own bank, Berkshire in iron and Buckinghamshire in timber. When the Buckinghamshire surveyor saw the Berkshire workmen on the boundary point and about to saw through the middle of the central arch, he obtained an injunction to prevent them 'cutting, severing or weakening the joists of the centre arch'. The matter then went to the Chancery Court, where both sides were ordered by the Lord Chancellor 'to proceed without impeding each other'. The resulting fourth bridge can be seen in a painting dated 1837 and another of 1850, the year before its final demise. At the uneasy central join, it appears that Berkshire had built a cantilevered structure which did not depend upon the Buckinghamshire half for its stability.

During the 18th century many houses in the High Street were built or rebuilt in the fashion of the time. This was partly due to changes in land use caused by the building of the bridge, and also to prosperity brought by trade and traffic using the toll-free bridge. In the Oram print of the first bridge, a cottage occupying the ancient ferry land is shown at the Datchet end of the bridge, probably belonging to the Hale family who had run the ferry business from there. At some time before 1780 this redundant ferry land had been sold by the Lord of the Manor to James Haydock who built the grand Datchet Lodge there. This house, which has been recently converted into flats, can be seen in two views of the second bridge.

James Haydock also owned the 16th-century buildings on the opposite corner, now called Old Bridge House and Post House, visible in prints of the second bridge. One, or both of these were licensed under the sign of the *White Horse* from 1726 until 1767, at a prime site for trading right at the foot of the bridge. The old *Rose*, or *Duke of Northumberland's Head*, ceased to be an alehouse in 1733, its trade very likely having suffered from competition with the *White Horse*. It became a carpenter's shop and then a butcher's, when a substantial new wing was added fronting the

42 The fourth bridge, 1837, from the Windsor side, by J. Bannister, showing the central join between the iron (Berkshire) and wood (Buckinghamshire) constructions.

43 The last view of the bridge, looking towards Datchet, by J. Chapman, *c.1850*.

road with a façade of chequered brickwork. Holiman's Plat (or St Helen's Cottage), almost opposite the new butcher's, was remodelled in similar chequered brick around an older timber-framed house. Next along on the same side, Clifton House and The Cottage were built about the middle of the century, occupied in the 1780s by the musician Richard Clark. Little Dene is rather later, and all three were new buildings in red brick, not remodellings of earlier ones. The Lord of the Manor also had a new house built on the other side of the road for renting out, at first used by the steward of the Manor. It is now the two shops at 6 and 8 High Street. The present *Morning Star* was another 18th-century rebuilding around the core of an older house, and the panelling in the room to the right of the entrance dates from the original building. It was a private house owned by the Dearle family, and not a beershop until the 1850s.

The Lords of the Manor and the Manor House

Lord Montagu of Beaulieu still maintains his family's connection with the Manor of Datchet, which began when John, Duke of Montagu, bought it in the middle of the 18th century. The way in which the Manor changed hands, by purchase or inheritance, can be difficult to grasp even when simplified, but the following brief account is given to establish the sequence of owners.

Both Datchet Manor and Ditton Park came into the Montagu family at about the same time but by different routes. At Datchet, Budd Wase, who had bought the manor from the Wheeler's heirs in 1680, left no heirs, and his niece Ann inherited it as an infant. Sir John Whitfield, who had been William Wheeler's steward, became guardian to the young Ann Wase and married her in 1723. John Whitfield was then Lord of the Manor until he sold it to Jonathan Smith in 1733, and in 1742 John,

44   Floods, in 1891, from *Manor Hotel* corner looking across to Rectory House; the two old houses left of centre were soon afterwards replaced by Barclays Bank and the Bank House.

45   Sir Robert Harvey's hunt meeting outside *The Manor Hotel*, by William Corden, 1874. The Harvey family lived at Langley Park from 1788 to the 1870s. The painter has emphasised the house in which he and his father lived, now 8 High Street, here seen before the shop fronts were added. The white building next on the corner is the old *White Hart* inn, by then a baker's shop. Beyond is the *Morning Star* with 'Temple's' tenements adjacent, now Temples Cottages. Beyond, projecting forward, is the Hammerson's blacksmith workshop, later Boot's hardware.

Duke of Montagu bought Datchet from him.

Ditton Park had been granted in 1615 to Sir Ralph Winwood, Secretary of State to James I and Charles I. Ralph Winwood's daughter Ann married Ralph, Lord Montagu of Boughton, and they inherited Ditton Park. He was created Duke of Montagu in 1705 and died in 1709, and his successor was John, Duke of Montagu, who bought Datchet. So from 1742 onwards, both Ditton Park and the Manor of Datchet were owned by the Montagu family and by that of the Dukes of Buccleuch to whom they were related by marriage.

Budd Wase's widow, Sarah, remained at Riding Court until her death in 1712. The estate is said to have been sold several times before being bought by John, Duke of Montagu at the same time as Datchet Manor, though separately. It then seems to have been reduced to the status of a manorial home farmstead and was tenanted by the Style family for many generations. From the 1740s the Montagus and then the Buccleuchs lived at the very grand Ditton Park, which was completely rebuilt after a serious fire in 1812. The village Manor House continued to be let to tenants. In the 1730s it is described as 'The House call'd The Mannor house, Lett at 16s.',

and it is known to have been divided into separate tenements by 1780. Both the main house and Manor Cottages were occupied by families of gentleman or yeoman status, the Aldridges, Ogilvys and Bradleys, whose tombstones dating from the 1690s are among the earliest in the churchyard. The cottages were given fashionable brick fronts and sash windows, leaving their timber frames almost untouched inside. But the Manor House itself was not modernised at the same time, perhaps because it had already been updated in the mid-17th century by the addition of a new wing.

The Needham Family, Datchet House and the Turnpike Road

Datchet House, in London Road just north of the church, was bought by the Needham family, Earls of Kilmorey, in the 1740s when Lady Kilmorey moved to Datchet from Iver. It is known that there has been a series of houses on this site since late medieval times, although the present house was probably built by the Needhams. In 1748 the long brick wall, which screens the grounds of the house from the road, was built on a strip of land leased by Lady Kilmorey from the Manor. Her orchard

46 Datchet House, London Road.

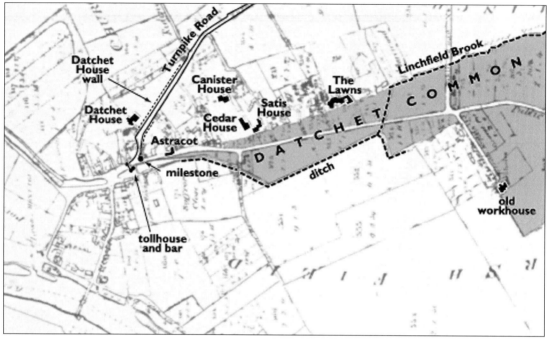

47   The Turnpike Road, Horton Road and Datchet Common, based on the 1834 enclosure map.

on the opposite side of the road was also walled in, suggesting that Datchet House's land had originally stretched right across the line of the road. This road, our present London Road, was late in developing as a main route, being recorded as 'Churchfield Lane' in 1667, but as 'the highway from Datchet to Colnbrook' in 1723. The timing strongly suggests that it was the free bridge which caused more traffic to use this shorter London Road way to the Bath Road, in preference to the original route along the Horton Road. Then in 1766 its developing status as a main road was confirmed when it was adopted by the Colnbrook Turnpike Trust.

During the first half of the 18th century roads across the country were being improved by the Turnpike Trusts, set up by private Acts of Parliament and raising their funds by charging tolls. The Trusts worked in a piecemeal fashion, each concerned only with its own defined stretch of road and intended as much to make a profit as to redesign and repair roads. Until

the advent of Turnpike Trusts, all roads, even the main highways, were the responsibility of the parish they ran through. An Act of 1555 had ordered 'overseers of the highways' to be appointed in each parish or town and every householder to work on the roads, or pay for another man to do so, for a number of 'statutory days' (four or six) in every year. All minor roads continued to be repaired by this means.

In 1727 the Colnbrook Trust was set up to improve the nine-mile section of road from Cranford Bridge to Maidenhead Bridge, part of the Bath Road or A4. Then in 1766 the trustees applied to parliament to take over two off-shoots from their main road, firstly the stretch from Slough to Eton followed by the road from Langley Broom past Ditton to Datchet Bridge, now our London Road. By 1768 plans were under way to improve the section passing through Ditton Green to Ashley's Corner (where the present Ditton Road meets London Road), which was in a dangerous condition. At that point Lord Kilmorey and Thomas Needham became trustees. The co-operation of the family over alterations around Datchet House was essential to the success of the road, and their presence on the Trust suggests they felt the upgrading of the road to be an advantage. The corner of Datchet House's wall was taken down and rebuilt further back from the line of the road, presumably where the wall abuts the churchyard, as it had protruded to make the carriageway there even narrower than it is at present. Sixteen years later this corner was widened again by taking down two cottages belonging to Mrs. Needham and a barn adjoining Church Cottage. This barn may have been on the site of James Cottages, built in 1853. it is no wonder that the old Churchfield Lane, twisting between walls and buildings, had not been used as a viable main route.

In 1768 the Trust recut their original milestones and added new ones on the two new cross roads. The 18th milestone out of London on the Bath Road is now stranded on a traffic island at junction 5 of the M4, while two new ones numbered 19 and 20 marked the way into Datchet. The 19th milestone was re-sited when the motorway was built but has recently disappeared, and the 20th survives precariously outside Church Cottage in the village centre. The toll gate was placed across the road from the *Royal Stag*, and a tiny toll house built just where the *Stag*'s sign post stands now, near the edge of the pool. (Both the toll gate and house were removed in the 1860s.) The turnpike road continued through the centre of Datchet to the foot of the Thames bridge, and thus included the High Street but not responsibility for the bridge over the pool, which continued to be maintained by the Barker Bridge Trust. There were frequent complaints about avoidance of tolls in Datchet, because a traveller arriving along the Horton Road and exiting along Back Lane or the lane to Slough used a few yards of turnpike road and passed through the toll gate. It was an unpopular

situation for both the inhabitants and travellers. Some road users were always exempt from turnpike charges; pedestrians, churchgoers on Sundays, funerals, mail coaches and some agricultural carts, while those living within a mile of a tollgate could make one annual payment.

The local nobility and gentry who acted as trustees met regularly to conduct business at local inns, and the Colnbrook Trustees often held their meetings at the *Castle Inn* near Salthill in Slough. It was there, in 1773, that the Hon. Thomas Needham was one of five trustees who died of a sudden severe illness after a Trust meeting and dinner there. Five others became seriously ill but recovered, and only one was completely unaffected. The event was the talk of London and reported in the newspapers, with conflicting theories spreading alarm. The landlady, Mrs. Partridge, and her cooking arrangements were at first suspected,

48 Milestone outside Church Cottage, London Road. The distances are: London 20 miles, Windsor 1 mile, Colnbrook 3 miles.

but attention was then drawn to the fact that before the Turnpike Trust meeting the trustees had considered the cases of several paupers, who were due to be returned to their own parishes. One of these had appeared very ill, and it was suspected he had an infection which the trustees had caught. On her deathbed many years later, Mrs. Partridge confessed that the turtle soup for the fatal day had been left standing overnight in a copper pan and that, when reheated, the bottom of it was green with verdigris. It had been a complete accident and the cook did not know of the danger. The Turnpike Trust minutes made no reference to the incident beyond recording the names of those who had 'recently died', and that in future only Turnpike business was to be conducted at their meetings. This implies that they blamed the sick pauper (who recovered), rather than the cook, and their meetings continued to be held at the *Castle Inn* in alternate years.[2]

Thomas Needham was the eldest son of John, Viscount of Kilmorey, and his accidental death at the age of 33 must have been a great blow to the family. Thomas's younger brother, Francis Jack, was also involved in local affairs at Datchet, becoming a trustee of the Barker Bridge House Trust in 1793. The following year he stated in the minutes of the Trust that he was leaving the country for military service in Ireland and formally relinquished his treasurer's post to the only other surviving trustee, James Haydock. Two of the other trustees had died, one was rendered speechless and another had gone to live in America. Francis Jack already had a distinguished career in the American War of Independence and in Ireland he was credited with saving Dublin at the Battle of Arklow. In 1822 he was created the first Earl of Kilmorey and did not return to Datchet but settled at the family's main estate in Shavington in Shropshire. His son, also Francis Jack, with his wife and eight daughters, took up residence again at Datchet House and the family remained there until the turn of the

20th century. The tomb slab which commemorates the earlier members of the family is in the chancel of the church, while more recent graves are in the churchyard between the church and Datchet House itself.

During this period, burial shrouds had to be made of woollen cloth under a law designed to protect the wool industry. A penalty was due for failure to comply, so that burial in linen became a mark of ability to pay the fine and hence of social superiority. In Datchet during the 18th century, the Needham and the Wase families were the only ones so conscious of their status that they took this last chance to declare it publicly. 'Buried in linnen and the 50 shilling fine paid' was added to the burial register entries for Sarah Wase and the Hon. Thomas Needham.

The Barker Bridge House Trust

Robert Barker is said to have founded the Bridge House Trust just before his death in 1645, but although he named the 17 inhabitants who were jointly to own it, the deed made no reference to the bridge nor its repair, for which Queen Elizabeth had originally given the Bridge House, or 'Churchlands'. Clearly this group of powerful men were functioning as trustees and using the profits to repair the bridge, but the purposes of the Trust were not formally established until 1724. In that year, the principal landowners and the overseers of the poor in Datchet brought a law suit to the Chancery Court after the death of Benjamin Lane, one of the last surviving trustees. He was found to have kept £128 17s. 5½d. of Trust money in a bag marked 'Datchet Bagg', and the Court was asked to establish the purposes for which this sum and all future money was to be used. It was recognised that Robert Barker had 'intended' a bridge to be built by his 1644 deed, and in 1724 (80 years later) it was assumed that the bridge had indeed been built through his gift. In fact the road bridge had certainly existed since at least 1565, and it was the footbridge between the church and the Manor

House which was erected on Robert Barker's instructions, perhaps during his lifetime. The Court also set up a more effective system for appointing and replacing trustees. From this date the Trust's minutes exist in an almost unbroken sequence and provide a great deal of information about the village in a period before any other parish records for Datchet survive.[3]

The Court deemed that in future the purposes of the Trust money were to be:

(1) To repair or new build the bridge and Bridge House.

(2) ... in regard the town and parish of Datchet lies in a low and watry country and the waters in times of great raines and floods overflow and run in many places ... and thereby incommode the inhabitants of Datchet not only in their way to and from their parish church but in their passages to their common fields and publick roads ... therefore the surplus of the money should be applyed ... to build or repair other bridges and causeways providing passages over such Churchways and watry places ...

(3) For repairing 'the houses called the parish almshouses'.

In effect, the Bridge Trust was taking on some of the responsibilities which would otherwise have fallen on the parish. The Trust had a constant source of money from the rent of the Bridge House and land, and by expending it in these ways the trustees are likely to have reduced the level of the parish rates paid by all householders, including themselves. The Trust's bridge almost certainly carried far more traffic through the village once the Thames bridge was built, and constantly needed money to be spent on it. The upkeep of the almshouse seems to be unconnected with the other 'watry' purposes, but the fact that the overseers of the poor took part in bringing the court case shows that the money was already being used in this way, perhaps as the church was so poor and the almshouse was adjacent to the Bridge House. (Confusion is now even greater since

the almshouse building is called 'The Bridge', while the actual Bridge House next door is known by its sign, the *Royal Stag*.)

The story of the Barker Bridge Trust is closely bound up with its chief asset, the Bridge House, then called the the *Five Bells*. Immediately after the court case of 1723 was settled, money was spent on major repairs to the bridge and the *Five Bells*, but by 1730 the first quarrel had broken out. John Herbert had spent Trust money without the consent of the other trustees, and had employed workmen at the *Five Bells* for his own purposes, he being the lessee. The Trust declined to pay these bills, as they were a 'manifest Violation and Abuse of the Trust', and the *Five Bells* was leased to a new tenant, Edmund Earley, at an increased rent.

Later in the same year the trustees were back in court over the case of the vicarage trees. The Bridge House land behind the pub abutted on to the vicarage, and the vicar

... complained very justly that the fence between the vicarage orchard and the garden belonging to the trust hath for several months lain down, to the great damage of the vicar's orchard by cattle and hogs trespassing there. He had often applied to the trustees to make up their fence, and they refuse to comply unless he consents to their fencing in a row of elm trees which he alleges belongs to his vicarage and not to the Trust.

A compromise was reached, whereby the trees were to be felled in order to pay for a new fence, but the incident is typical of the litigiousness of both the Trust and the people it dealt with during the 18th century.

In 1733 the trustees took legal advice over problems with the new Lord of the Manor, Jonathan Smith, who was 'making interruptions and encroachments which render less effectual the due executions of their Trust'. The next year the minutes recorded that, 'The church footways [paths used for travel to church, not the paths in the church-yard] are out of repair by recent floods and

49   Tombstone of Edmund Earley (d. 1770), Datchet churchyard.

by Mr. Smith narrowing them by digging trenches to the great annoyance of the parishioners'. In 1737 things were worse, 'Mr. Smith having pulled down the front of the room erected by Edmund Earley, tenant to the Bridge House, upon a presumption that Earley had carried his wall out too far and had thereby encroached on the waste'. (The 'waste' was common land of the Manor, including small portions in front of private properties.) The trustees 'ordered that the wall be pulled down and rebuilt on the old foundations and that the cost of rebuilding be allowed to Mr. Earley, the expense to the Trustees caused by this Act of Violence amounting to 10s.'.

The Bridge House Trustees were not only engaged in a constant and expensive battle with Datchet's 'watry places', and with the rebuilding of the almshouse when it was beyond repair, but were also dealing with their own recalcitrant tenant at the *Five Bells*. Edmund Earley came from an extraordinarily quarrelsome family who were gentlemen horse-dealers and

wealthy owners of properties along the Horton Road. In 1747 the minutes reported that:

> Edmund Earley has not complied with his agreement to build new stables and lodging rooms, nor has he made any improvements about the premises but suffers them to run to ruin. He has insulted and abused the Trustees for not pulling down the almshouses out of his way, and he suffers his own menservants to ride their horses on the parish footways to the great annoyance of the inhabitants and in defiance of the Trustees.

The trustees decided to insist he must be legally bound to good behaviour before renewing his tenancy. Earley leased *The Five Bells* but did not run the inn himself; his undertenant had been John Jones, but from 1764 the publican was John Quick who was married to Ann Earley. She was probably Edmund's daughter, and good behaviour prevailed from then on, with Ann herself being the Licensed Victualler from Edmund's death in 1770 through the 1780s. After 1764 major repairs and rebuilding were done at the *Five Bells*, so it may be that Edmund Earley was deliberately causing trouble in order to place his own relative as tenant there. Another member of the family, Joshua Earley, appeared at the County Court in Aylesbury in 1794 accused of the most extraordinary theft. He had 'taken and unjustly detained' all the household goods belonging to George Gosden, these goods being detailed in Court:

> Three bay horses, one grey horse, one poney, horse cloths, a cow, saddle & bridle, dung, lumber, two pigs, poultry, straw, a one horse chaise & harness, a market cart & harness, faggotts & wood, a ladder, a cow crib, a wheelbarrow, brewing utensils, a large copper, styes, a horse trough, four bins of corn, hay and all the other goods, stock, and effects upon, in or about the premises of George Gosden situate at Datchet.

How did Joshua Earley manage to remove everything from Gosden's house and, more significantly, why should he want to? George Gosden was the occupier of one of Joshua's properties along the Horton Road, so they could have disagreed about rent or tenancy, although both were horsedealers, a business with a reputation for sharp practices. George Gosden was also a huntsman to George III and a Yeoman Pricker, a light horseman who had responsibility for protecting the king while he was hunting. Gosden died in 1844 at the age of 91 and is buried at Langley. Edmund Earley's tombstone in the churchyard at Datchet is carved with beautiful classical figures and motifs, demonstrating both the wealth and fashionable taste of his family.

Jonathan Smith had been in trouble at the Manor Court in 1729, before he became Lord of the Manor himself. He had '... made severall encroachments upon the waste, especially for not filling up a trench he hath dug upon the common, to the manifest injury of the inhabitants, which trench is near 100 yards long, seven feet wide and five feet deep'. What was Jonathan Smith doing? His own explanations are never heard, only the complaints of others. It is known that he bought a house belonging to Benjamin Lane in the Horton Road, and acquired adjacent plots of land in order to build his new Canister House. (This was the predecessor of the later Leigh House, itself now gone.) Another house owner along this strip also dug trenches and carried off soil at about the same time, and one theory is that these powerful property holders were reshaping the lie of the land to their own

advantage. The 1834 enclosure map suggests that the road has been moved further south at some time, as all the property boundaries were then shown as being north of it by about the same amount, and as having a strip of common between their gardens and the road. (The Enclosure Act tidied this up by awarding each section of common to the individual house-holder on its north.) Was the road being rebuilt around 1730, or were they diverting the stream further away from their homes? Trenches of the size recorded are likely to have made a permanent impression on the landscape, and could even be the present ditch across the recreation ground. It must have come as some relief in 1742 when Jonathan Smith sold the Manor to the Duke of Montagu, although he did not relinquish all his interests here; his Canister House was occupied by Anne, Duchess of Hamilton and then by his own daughter, Justine.

Canister House was built in the 1760s on a large plot of land bought from Benjamin Lane 'near to the house of John Dell'. This house of Dell's still exists as the 17th-century Cedar House, lying back in a long garden from Horton Road. It is the only surviving house of those known to have been owned by the Earley family, who had bought both Canister House and its much older neighbour by 1780. Cedar House was not, strictly speaking, a dower house, although it was a subsidiary of the grander new Canister. The Dell family was a powerful local

50 Cedar House, Horton Road. Although much altered, this timber-framed house dates back to at least the 17th century.

presence, as John Dell farmed both the lands of the Manor, which he leased from John Whitfield, and the Lascelles estates at Southlea. He was a Bridge House Trustee, and his father Thomas had leased the rectory from St George's. The house now called Astracot, part of the rectory's property, was occupied by William Earley, son of Edmund, until the early 1800s. At some time during the 18th century the house was fashionably updated by the addition of its present brick façade and sash windows, which might have been carried out by William Earley.

Two pieces of local folklore are associated with the Bridge Trust's inn, the *Royal Stag*, which is said to be haunted by various apparitions. Earlier this century, a broken tombstone was unearthed in the yard which commemorated one William Herbert, a wealthy maltster, who died in 1705. William was the father of John Herbert, the licensee who caused such trouble for the Trust. There have been suggestions of sinister reasons for the stone being broken, but the truth is probably more prosaic. The churchyard is known to have been reduced in size more than once on the London Road corner, where there are several other Herbert graves just inside the wall, and this one may have been damaged in resiting it. Behind the church, the boundary between the graveyard and the inn yard has also been moved, and the stone could easily have come to rest on the wrong side. However, there is no explanation for the ghostly handprint of a child which is said to appear on one of the downstairs window panes on the churchyard side. Unless its manifestation is a hoax, it defies rational explanation, but there is no evidence to confirm the tale of a child dying in the churchyard waiting for her father to come out of the pub. This is modern folklore, and of recent origin, but does not prevent speculation about supernatural happenings at the *Royal Stag* being enjoyed. The *Manor Hotel* does not have a reputation for being haunted, but it is often said that one of the downstairs rooms was used

in the past as a mortuary. This is quite true and not at all unusual. Until the end of the 19th century the coroner would come to the scene of any suspicious death, conducting his inquest and viewing the body at the chief inn of a village or town. Until quite recently there was an extremely old barn in Queen's Road, lately a boat hiring business, which is also said to have been used as a mortuary during a smallpox epidemic. There is as yet no evidence for this, but it is possible.

William Herschel in Datchet

William Herschel and his sister Caroline spent three years in Datchet from 1782 in a house in Horton Road. It has been said that Satis House, demolished in the 1970s, was Herschel's home, but new evidence from the Land Tax listings shows that it was not, although that house did exist at the time. From 1783 to 1785, 'Mr. Herschell' was the occupier of a house further east along the road, part of a complex of buildings later called the Lawn and owned by Mr. Reddington, a wealthy Windsor brewer. Several separate dwellings existed there as wings added to a house originally built in the 16th century. Most of these old buildings, including the part rented by the Herschels, were pulled down during a major remodelling in the 1850s. What is left today includes a splendid 18th-century staircase and drawing room, known to have been in existence when Herschel lived in the adjacent house. In the gardens behind the Lawn, where Herschel erected his telescope, an ice house still exists. It is a typical 18th-century brick vaulted chamber, just below ground level and covered by a mound of earth for insulation. This phase of the building, developing the much older house, was probably carried out by the Parr family who owned it before William Reddington.

The chief source of information about Herschel's life is his sister Caroline's diary, in which she describes their 'new house or ... rather, the ruins of a place which had once served as a hunting seat to some gentleman and had not

51 *Above left*. Satis House, before demolition in 1970. The name 'Satis' dates from fairly recent times, and must be a reference to Miss Haversham's house in Charles Dickens' *Great Expectations*.

52 *Above right*. The Lawn, ballroom wing.

53 *Right*. Eighteenth-century icehouse in the garden of the Lawn, showing brick-vaulted chamber below ground level.

54 *Below*. The 20-foot telescope in a garden in Datchet, almost certainly at the back of the Lawn.

55 Portrait of William Herschel. Print of original engraving by Ryder after Abbott.

56 Portrait of Caroline Herschel in old age.

been inhabited for years'. The Herschels arrived at Datchet from Bath on 1 August 1782, staying the night at the *Five Bells* and watching the wagons arrive safely the next morning with all their telescope tubes and instruments. During the 1780s William was engaged in building larger and better telescopes and in his duties as Astronomer Royal to George III. He had first observed the planet Uranus through the seven-foot telescope when in Bath, and he used this to demonstrate his discoveries to the king during his visits to Windsor at night. His Datchet house had a long grass plot behind it where a 20-ft. telescope was built, preceding the great 40-ft. one constructed at Slough. Caroline was not at all happy in Datchet, and William was often ill. Caroline's journal details her complaints as well as their work:[4]

> The greatest hindrance towards making ourselves comfortable was our having brought no servant with us, for my brother had engaged one to be ready to receive us, but on enquiring it was found she was in prison for theft, and for a fortnight I could not get a sight of any woman but the wife of the Gardener [He proved to be a very steady attendant at night at the working handle of the telescope, until he died of smallpox]. This old woman could be of no further service to me than shewing me the shops, and the first time I went to make markets I was astonished at the dearness of every article and saw at once that my brother's scheme of living cheaply in the country on eggs and bacon would come to nothing; for at Bath I had the week before bought from 16 to 20 eggs for 6d., here I could get no more than five for 4d. Butchers' meat was dearer and the only butcher at Datchet would besides not give honest weight and we were obliged to deal, all the time we lived there, at Windsor.' [This butcher was Stevens, at no. 20 High Street.]

William was working at a frantic pace to build the 20ft telescope himself, aided practically by Caroline who was a distinguished astronomer in her own right. He decided to save time by having some parts of the instruments made by a retired watchmaker living on Datchet

Common, probably at an old house at the top of Holmlea Road. But, in Caroline's words, 'the work was so bad and the charges so unreasonable that he could not be employed'. However, the carpenters and smiths of Datchet were all 'in daily requisition', making machinery and the supporting structure, which fell down at least once as William climbed up to use it before the ladders were completed.

The winter of 1783 was extremely hard and one night Caroline ripped open her leg on a butcher's hook covered by snow, although she was stoically back at her post recording William's observations within a few nights. William put the severe weather to good use, giving scientific papers on the effects of moisture, fog and frost on telescopic vision. William's son, John, later wrote of his father's time at Datchet: 'When the waters were out round his garden, he used to rub himself all over with a raw onion to keep off the infection of the ague, which was then prevalent; however, he caught it at last'. Although William was said to have an excellent constitution, he was extremely ill after three winters at Datchet, and a change of residence to a drier spot was recommended by his physician. In 1785 they moved to Clay Hall at Old Windsor, and then again in 1786 to Slough where he spent the rest of his life.

At about the same period, two other famous women appear to have resided briefly at Datchet. Samuel Osborn wrote that 'Perdita' (Mary Robinson), the beautiful actress admired by the future George IV when Prince of Wales, lived at the house close to the walled enclosures at Southlea. Her husband's name was Thomas, and a Thomas Robinson did occupy this house in the years after Mary's death, so the tradition of her presence here is supported by some evidence, however slight. The other intriguing name is Mrs. Dora Jordan who was the mistress of the Duke of Clarence, later William IV. In 1794 she was listed as the occupier of a house in Datchet, the very same year in which she was hissed off the London stage in a play written by 'Perdita'.[5]

The Rectory, the Church, and the Dissenters

John Dell, the owner of Cedar House, also leased the rectory properties from St George's from 1685 to 1699, when Ralph Bragg of Eton became rector. Ralph died in 1715 and the rectory passed to Christopher Arnold. He must have been related by marriage to the Bragg family, as a John Bragg-Arnold was brought from London for burial at Datchet. Christopher Arnold's church memorial describes him as Citizen and Goldsmith of London, and it is positioned just above that of Richard Hanbury who bore the same titles. Arnold was a partner of Henry Hoare, a City banker, and the continuity of interests suggests that Datchet remained well known and favoured among the City's banking community. The rectory continued to be held by relatives of the Arnold family, passing to Frances and Rosalind Marshall in 1773 and then to James Russell, Arnold's son-in-law, in 1787. Russell spent £1,200, a huge amount of money, on rebuilding the Rectory House, and died insolvent in 1793. The lease was then renewed to Mrs. Russell and her daughters at a lower sum than usual because of her husband's expenditure. The eldest of these daughters was married to John Richards, who became Datchet's rector from 1800 and played a significant part in many of the village's affairs.

Christopher Arnold's wife, Mary, died aged 82 in 1770, leaving a bequest to poor housekeepers of £110 in shares, the income to be distributed on Christmas Day. The inscription on the Arnolds' memorial describes Christopher as 'Of most unblemished reputation and simplicity of life; In business distinguished for assiduity, integrity and honour'. His widow, Mary, is praised for 'Her piety, secret and extensive charities ... her affability and cheerfulness'. In the following decades, Francis and Rosamund Marshall each left £100 in annuities to be distributed by the vicar and churchwardens to those of the poor not receiving parish relief. These bequests are typical of the 18th century, a period when the church actively promoted charitable giving, but strictly under the control of the parish authorities. In an increasingly secular society the maintenance of social order seems to have been of more concern to the Church of England than the spiritual welfare of the people. These legacies, together with several others, have since been amalgamated as Datchet United Charities and still provide for the elderly, sick, and needy as they were originally intended to do.

Following the disastrous series of vicars in the middle of the 17th century, Thomas Jenkinson was appointed vicar in 1682 and remained here for an incredible 60 years. Although there were no dramatic improvements during this time, at least the parish was in the care of a more stable individual who was better paid; several gifts from Windsor after the Restoration having more than doubled the stipend. In 1706 Thomas Jenkinson replied to the Archdeacon of Buckinghamshire's question-naire, describing his parish in the following words:

> No person of quality or estate lives here. Mrs. Sarah Wase, a widow and Lady of the Manor lives in the parish and last July gave a silver flagon and plate to be used at the communion. [These are still in use.] Mr. Benjamin Lane lives here, the rest are all of a mean condition [i.e. poor]. The parish is of a small extent, containing about fifty families. There is no papist or reputed papist and no dissenter of any kind or any meeting house. There is a poor woman that teaches children to read and say their catechism. There is a small alm-shouse of seven rooms into which they put such of their poor parishioners as cannot pay rent, and the parish keep it in repair [Now 'The Bridge'].

Jenkinson, writing in 1706, could describe Datchet as having only two 'persons of quality', but it has already been shown that by the middle of the century there were fashionable new buildings or remodellings of old houses, and around a dozen families of some wealth and

status. This may be further evidence for new prosperity brought by the building of the Thames bridge.

The church building itself reflected the continuing poor state of parish finances. A drawing of 1787 is the first known depiction of the building and shows a barn-like nave with a lower chancel, a south porch and a low tower over the west end of the north aisle. It had not been rebuilt since the 14th century, and was only kept in repair with difficulty. There were five bells in the tower, as the name of the adjacent Bridge House suggests, the earliest dating from 1607. They still exist in the new tower although one has been replaced and another recast. Until the whole church was rebuilt in the 1850s, the only improvements to it were made by James Randall, a parish foundling who was in service all his life as footman and coachman to the Drew family at the Lawn in Horton Road. He was described as 'A small, dark, shrunken looking man, very peculiar, as were Mrs. and Miss Drew'. In 1818 he built a vestry, the church not having had one previously, beyond the west end of the nave, and he was buried beneath it in 1823 at his own request. In the year before he died he provided the church with money to buy a clock and the mechanism is still working today, re-sited in the new tower.

In 1785 a group of Protestant Dissent-ers, calling themselves Independents, registered their assembly with the Bishop of Lincoln. Their Meeting House was at first a barn in the High Street, part of John Fleetwood Marsh's farm homestead, of which only Goodwyn House survives. The Baptist Chapel was built on the site of this barn in 1841, and the building still exists as the three shops and flats beside the level crossing. The Marsh family were wealthy yeoman farmers, tenants of the Bridge House lands and the rectory and Eton College estates. Daniel Marsh, John Fleetwood's father, had married Ellen Style in an alliance which consolidated their farming

57 St Mary's Church in 1787.

58 St Mary's Church, showing clock and spire added to the tower. At the left is the *Royal Stag* before the new front block was added; on the right is Datchet House.

59 Tombstone of George Hale (d. 1838).

interests, as the Style family tenanted Riding Court Farm from the Lord of the Manor. In 1794 John Fleetwood Marsh emigrated to America, but left an endowment for the use of the baptist minister. The family may have been divided by religion, since Daniel Marsh left a bequest of bread for the poor through the churchwardens of the parish church. A 'Mr. Marsh' also owned Church Cottage from the 1760s to the 1790s. This was probably John Fleetwood, as the property was bought by one of the tenants, Mrs. Lamb, in 1795, the year after John left for America. In 1816

George Hale the farrier bought the house, although it seems that he was running his business at the workshops on the corner by about 1800. He died in 1838 and his tombstone, embellished with the tools of his trade, stands overlooking the churchyard wall and facing Church Cottage. He appears to have been related to the Hales, who were recorded in Datchet from before 1400 and ran the ferry for two hundred years. George had no sons and his descendants, whose graves also face their house, were at first named Hale-Pearce and then just Pearce.

The Workhouse and the Poor

The little almshouse building ('The Bridge') had been a parish poorhouse since Elizabethan times, when parishes were made responsible for their own paupers through the election of 'overseers of the poor' and the levying of a local poor rate on householders. During the 18th century, and particularly after an Act of 1782, local workhouses were established to deal with growing numbers of able-bodied poor as well as the old and sick. These were not intended to be punitive as were the 'Union' workhouses established after 1834, but aimed to provide employment for those who could work as well as shelter for those who could not. Until 1834 the poor were also allowed to be 'relieved' by the parish while staying on in their own homes, only the oldest, most sick or destitute being admitted to the workhouse which was never a pleasant option. When Datchet's workhouse was built in about 1790, on the Common at the far end of the modern Holmlea Road, it made the village centre poorhouse redundant. It was let out as a dwelling house and then from 1820 as a shop, with its rent used towards the upkeep of the poor and thus reducing the rate paid by everyone else.

The operation of the workhouse was let out to a contractor, as was usually the case, and the leasing agreement drawn up between the parish officers and Stephen Riddington in 1795 has survived. The overseers of the poor stipulated that for dinners the inmates should have 'good, sweet, sound and wholesome roast or boiled beef or mutton, with good wheaten bread and small ale without stint', and that they should sit together at meals and eat at their own discretion until satisfied. The children were to be taught to read and say their catechism and say grace before and after meals. A man was also employed 'to take care that the children behave themselves quiet in the Church every Sunday'. It is doubtful whether the reality of life for the paupers actually met these good intentions, but those overseeing their support were local people who knew them and there seems to have been genuine concern for their welfare.

Stephen Riddington was able to use the inmates' labour for his own profit, and the agreement describes the many textile processes that Riddington, a woollen manufacturer, intended to have carried out there. Wool was to be sorted, combed and spun, cloth and blankets were to be woven and stockings knitted. There is no further record of Riddington's business (and the workhouse had changed hands by 1800), but elsewhere such pauper labour was seldom a success. However, in 1825, the workhouse inmates were still required to cut the thistles (or probably teazles, still growing there abundantly), on the Common and the Forty, which were used commercially for combing the surface of woollen cloth. The poor law papers record two men who were basket makers. (They were standing surety for another, the father of a bastard child and liable to pay maintenance.) However, the occupation of these two men is the only evidence for basket making in Datchet, so it may be that the osiers grown along the river banks and riverside eyots were mainly supplied to other places.

The poor laws were still strictly applied, parish relief being given only to those who had established their right of 'settlement', and others were sent quickly back to their home parishes if they threatened to become a charge on the poor rates. Nationally, this led to large numbers of stray people who did not want to return to their place of origin and had no right of settlement anywhere else. They were effectively lost to society except when an inconvenient birth or death was recorded by the parish in which the event occurred. Thomas Jenkinson often noted such circumstances in his entries in the parish registers in the first half of the century. Over the period, a dozen people 'whose name we knew not' were buried, several of whom had drowned and were taken from the river here. In the 1740s, vagrants were classified according to the degree of threat they posed to society, and Jenkinson made clear distinctions between travellers, vagrants and vagabonds, even among those who were unknown or already dead. In the first half of the century 20 babies were born to vagabonds or vagrants within the parish, and many more mothers must have been hurried across the parish boundaries to avoid a chargeable birth and baptism.

Several stories are particularly poignant. In 1732, 'a new born female child was found laid in a basket at a door in our parish early in the morning, she was brought to Morning Prayer and was baptised and named Anne'. The next day Anne's burial was recorded. A very similar story was told in 1739, when a 'strange woman brought a female child into our parish and left it at the bridgefoot, which child was baptised in our church the next Sunday and named Jenner'; she also died the day after. A rather different case was that of 'Elizabeth Jervaise, an impudent strumpet, who was delivered of a male child, baptised Christopher on 23rd May 1732'. Christopher appears to have survived, or at least did not die in this parish. Two women, each described as 'a harlot', had children baptised in the 1730s, but whether they lived here or were passing through is not known.

Jenkinson also commented on sexual irregularity, as vicars had often done in the past; Richard Aston, gentleman, had two natural children baptised in 1705, both buried a week later. In 1713 at the baptism of John Rutter, a bastard, Jenkinson's memorandum states that John Rutter the father debauched his daughter-in-law, Susanna. She also seems to be the mother of John Rance, buried in 1724, 'the natural son of John Rance by his daughter in law, Susanna Rutter'. From 1700 to 1750, six natural children or bastards belonging to the parish were recorded, but from then until 1800 there were 15 described as baseborn or illegitimate. This curious increase reflects a significant rise in national statistics. A number of social factors have been suggested to account for the rise but it is not yet fully explained. The numbers of abandoned infants, usually illegitimate, led to the opening of Thomas Coram's Foundling Hospital in London. Many of these children were boarded out in the country and, although the arrival of those sent here was not recorded, their deaths frequently were. Six 'infants from London' were buried in the 1760s, three of them with the same family name.

Enclosure of the Land, 1810 to 1834

Enclosure was the process by which land held in the common fields, and cultivated communally, was converted to individually owned and managed land in enclosed plots. While land remained unenclosed, the 'rights of common' belonging to manorial tenants allowed grazing and gleaning after harvests, while the fields were manured by the stock feeding on them. There were clear advantages to be gained in being able to farm a compact area near to the farmstead and without reference to other owners. At the time, improvements in agricultural methods and commercial results were seen to be dependent upon enclosing. In Datchet the chief landowners had already consolidated their estates so that by 1780 most of the land belonged to only five farms and some of their smaller fields had already been enclosed. However, many parcels of land managed by these farmers remained scattered in the old open fields and there were still commons where cottagers had ancient rights to graze animals.

In some parts of the country, enclosure had already occurred gradually or by agreement, but, like thousands of other places, the process in Datchet was started by a private Act of Parliament which was passed in 1810. The final 'award', which mapped and recorded the ownership of the redistributed 'allotments' of land, was not drawn up until 1834, an unusually long delay. The explanation may lie partly in the death of both the commissioner appointed to administer the Act, and of the surveyor who valued and mapped the estates, so that new appointments had to be made during the process. The enclosure map and the details of the plots of land in the award are two of the most useful sources for the history of Datchet, particularly since few other records at parish level have survived.

The owners of the greatest amounts of land had to agree to the Enclosure Bill being initiated, and these were the Duchess of Buccleuch, as Lady of the Manor, and Edward Lascelles, Baron Harewood. (The Lascelles estate originated as the property accumulated by Christopher and Robert Barker.) The third major factor involved was the final extinction of the tithes which belonged to St George's Chapel, and through them to John Richards as rector. Tithes were not always dealt with at enclosure but, where they were, an allotment of land was made in compensation for final loss of tithe. The dean and canons of St George's Chapel were entitled by law to allotments equal to a fifth of all the arable land in the parish, and an eighth of all other previously titheable land. They then rented out the farming of this land, to obtain an income from it, to John Richards the rector who in his turn sublet to tenants.

John Richards was a battler for rights, including his own. He interfered in the redistribution of land, probably contributing to the delay in finalising the enclosure award, and continued to argue over the rent charged by St George's for their new estate. On the other hand, he pleaded eloquently for reduction of the rent during a period of severe weather and dreadful floods leading to a series of disastrous harvests around 1820. He had reduced the rent of his under-tenants to a minimum because no one could pay and the land was taking years to recover. His stream of irascible letters to St George's presents a picture of agricultural depression and despair through to the 1830s.

There were also many small and medium sized land-holdings which belonged to property owners from the time when all householders farmed strips of land in the open fields and held rights of common. After the chief landowners' plots were established, smaller allotments were made to other owners in proportion to the size of their original holdings. Few of these people actually wanted to farm their new plots of land and so, as their allotments usually lay beside a road for ease of access, many were eventually sold for the building of houses. In this way, enclosure enabled the village to develop beyond its old centre. The enclosure commissioners were also charged with rationalising roads and public footpaths, making new ones where necessary. Ditton Road is a completely new road made at this time; it is the straightest road in the parish and typical of enclosure commissioners' work.

It was possible to buy land speculatively in the years before enclosure, in anticipation of it taking place. Some owners were prepared to sell land as their tenants' rents were fixed at low prices and there was little profit to be made during bad times. One family in Datchet can be seen apparently taking advantage of this situation. John Goodwin, with his sons John and Ralph, seems to have arrived here as tenants of the Lord of the Manor's Ditton Farm, and in the 1780s owned both the old *Rose* and 'Goodwyn House' in the High Street. They were first described as butchers, but from the 1790s to 1810 rapidly acquired a great deal of land of their own as well as farming parts of the estates belonging to the Lascelles family and the rectory as well as the manor. Successful farmers had often grown to such powerful positions before, but this time there was more at stake. At enclosure the Goodwins were allotted the fourth largest estate after the three great landowners, and considerably more than any other ordinary owner. The farmhouse bearing their name mostly dates from John Goodwin's prestigious rebuilding in the 1800s. Their high profile presence did not last long, as by 1875 the lack of heirs and a family dispute over inheritance led to the property being divided and sold.

60 Goodwyn House, High Street.

Datchet's Enclosure Act was passed during the peak period for such Acts, at the time of the Napoleonic Wars (1793-1815) when grain prices were high, food was short, and farmers were anxious to bring the marginal land of the commons into arable production. It was also a period of great hardship and shortage, with labourers' wages too low to buy the expensive bread. A drastic measure was recommended to Buckinghamshire parishes in 1795; at the same time as suggesting that parishes should provide meat at reduced prices to compensate for the bread shortage, poor families were to have their dogs destroyed as a condition of being offered relief. The view of historians is that the smallest land holders and those dependent on rights of common suffered most by being dispossessed at enclosure, but evidence about the situation of these people both before and after the event is generally lacking. In Datchet* the 'peasant farmer' class had disappeared long before, but disruptive behaviour among the labouring poor at the time suggests that they were at the very least made alarmed and anxious by the hard times nationally and threatening changes locally.

Black Datchet

Writing in 1886, Samuel Osborn said that the village in the early years of the century was known as Black Datchet, because of the number of bad characters living here. This is borne out by the fact that one building of the county jail at Aylesbury was called the Datchet Wing, filled mostly with poachers. By the early 1800s the game laws had become increasingly severe and those caught were more likely to be imprisoned than previously. Although the sale of game birds was illegal before 1831, there was actually a flourishing trade in opposition to the rights of the landowners, and the number of poachers from Datchet suggests that they may have been operating in organised gangs trading through middlemen, not just stealing for their own family cooking pots. During the 1780s Benjamin Earley was the gamekeeper to the Earl of Buccleuch for the two manors, and he was followed in 1806 by William Scott, already the bailiff of the manors. After 1831 the laws were relaxed and poaching became a risky rural sport rather than a serious running battle.

Authority was being challenged in other ways, too. In 1812, 18 labouring men were

WHEREAS I, GEORGE OGILWY, have frequently given just cause of offence to the Rev. I. Phillips, both by my behaviour and by my language, for which Mr. Phillips expressed his forgiveness of me in words, the meaning of which I misunderstood; I do now humbly ask Pardon of Mr. Phillips for the same ; and I do faithfully promise, that in future I will be more circumspect in every part of my behaviour towards him, and more attentive to the discharge of my duty as Clerk of the parish of Datchet

Witness my Hand,
GEORGE OGILWY.

In the presence of us —
   John Goodwin, Jun.
   William Cooper, jun.
15th May, 1813.

61 *Windsor & Eton Express,* 1813, statements and counter-statements.

PARISH OF DATCHET.

WE, the undersigned, whose Names were attached to an Advertisement published in the WINDSOR EXPRESS of last week, purporting to be the ACKNOWLEDGMENT of GEORGE OGILWY, for his improper conduct to the Rev. James Phillips, hereby declare that the said document was drawn up by the Rev. Dr. Foster Pigott, and witnessed by us, with a view to the *private satisfaction alone* of the Rev. James Phillips, as the first step towards a general reconciliation of the Parish ; and that the said acknowledgment was published by the Rev. James Phillips without our knowledge or consent, and contrary to the intention with which the document was witnessed and approved of by us.

                                             JOHN GOODWIN, Jun.
Datchet, May 22, 1813.   WM. COOPER, Jun.

I, GEORGE OGILWY, do hereby declare the Oath I took on the 19th day of April last, before Sir Charles Palmer, was the truth ; in which is stated I did ask forgiveness at the Communion Table in Datchet Church, of the Rev. James Phillips, who answered he never would forgive me; and my Apology that was on Sunday last published in the Windsor Paper, had no concern with my Oath.

May 22, 1813.   GEORGE OGILWY.

taken for trial to Aylesbury, accused of assault, riots and conspiracy. Their victim was the curate, James Phillips, who was in dispute with the parish clerk, George Ogilwy. A quarrel seems to have arisen over a burial, which led to the dismissal of Ogilwy from his post. Phillips then found him still occupying his clerk's seat below the pulpit and removed him. For some obscure reason, the village rabble took Ogilwy's side and hounded the curate with 'rough music', a traditional way of expressing a community's disapproval. For many nights, and particularly on Sundays, a crowd of labourers lay in wait for him outside the blacksmith's shop adjacent to Church Cottage. They made a rowdy noise with horns and tin kettles and taunted him as 'the black dog' who had pulled 'the badger' (Ogilwy) out of his 'hole', his seat in the church. They had a stuffed badger skin on a pole which they paraded around the village, hollering, 'Where's the parson? Where's the black dog with the white collar?' The gang also terrified Phillips' female servant, calling, 'Here's the brindled bitch that lies at night with the black dog!' John Richards, the rector, wrote a reproving letter to Pond, the ringleader, which Pond read and laughed at openly in the street. Another of them was caught by Lord Montagu himself and taken into the house of William Scott the steward of the manor (6, High Street), where he instantly, but perhaps temporarily, became very contrite.

It seems that the gang was genuinely feared in the village. Few would give evidence for or against, or even identify the culprits. When Phillips took two of them before a magistrate he refused to act but required the curate to pay the men their day's lost wages. In his summing up at the end of the trial, the Chairman of the Court declared that, '... the prisoners' conduct had appeared so malignant that they could not bring, even from their own degraded village, one person to speak for their character.' Although Phillips had been curate for 14 years, he may have been generally unpopular and the whole village was perhaps in some way complicit, tolerating or turning a blind eye to events. Only nine of the accused were found guilty, but they received prison sentences of several months.

The precise origins of the quarrel and the ways in which it divided the village are now impossible to reconstruct fully, but there does seem to have been a continuing resentment against the pillars of the established church, which was expressed in acts of violence during the following years. In 1813 John Richards, a man likely to make himself unpopular, threatened to sue the parish officers for serious and deliberate damage done to trees in his plantation, the remnants of which now surround Churchmead School. Since he was paid £18 in compensation, responsibility of some sort must have been accepted, although at the same time the vestry meeting decided to charge him for a number of loads of gravel he had taken for private use from the parish gravel pit. Then in 1816 great alarm was caused by two burglaries, at the houses of Isaac Gosset the vicar and James Phillips the curate, who had apparently resumed his post. The motive seems to have been intimidation rather than theft; a gun was used threateningly but only trivial items were taken and abandoned nearby, Phillips having already removed his valuables from his house. A huge reward of £50 was offered for information about each offence but no one was ever caught. Alarm was great, and a meeting of the inhabitants was called at which a nightly patrol of the village was established by two persons armed with pistols and cutlasses. It is little wonder that the village was known as Black Datchet, and it was said that youths from the adjacent parishes would not cross the boundaries due to fear of Datchet's gangs.

Chapter Five

Railway and Revival:
Later 19th and Early 20th Centuries

Between the accession of Queen Victoria in 1837 and the outbreak of war in 1914, Datchet changed more radically than at any time before or since. While our current concerns may seem totally of our own age, many have their origins in Victorian times, including the arrival of the motor car. Datchet also exemplifies many of the technological innovations and social values which are typical of the Victorians. Almost all aspects of the village were in need of rethinking and ripe for change after the low point of the early 19th century. Even the characteristic visual appearance of the village centre is chiefly a product of the Victorian period. Robert Barker's Bridge Trust, after 200 years of repairing bridges, settled on the radical solution of culverting the stream underground which led to the creation of Datchet's village greens. To Victorian engineering we owe the arrival of the railway, causing reorganisation of the roads and bridges, and eventually also our constant traffic delays. For the first time, the village and its people become visible to us, both through photography and the decennial censuses which, from 1841, give the name, age and occupation of everyone here, allowing detailed reconstruction of families and their dwellings. In 1999, the longest living memory actually reached back into the last years of Victoria's reign, in a village which the Queen herself knew well.

The Lords of the Manor

Still at the pinnacle of Datchet society were the Duke and Duchess of Buccleuch and their family, residing in isolated splendour at Ditton Park, where Queen Victoria was a frequent visitor. In 1813, after a serious fire, the house and its chapel were rebuilt by Lady Elizabeth Montagu, wife of Henry Scott, 3rd Duke of Buccleuch, but she gave the use of it to her second son, Henry James, Lord Montagu of Boughton. After his death in 1845, the estate passed to his nephew, Walter Francis, 5th Duke of Buccleuch and, when he died in 1884, Ditton was used as her dower house by the Duchess.

At last, in the 1870s, the Lord of the Manor took an active interest in the Manor House. Since the late 18th century it had quietly mouldered away, divided into multiple tenancies housing artisan families and old manorial servants, with parts converted for the poor and for a school. As demand increased in the village for higher status dwellings to rent, the old building was renovated, divided into two houses, and given a dramatic mock Jacobean timbered façade. This bears very little relation either to the original exterior or to the genuine timber-framed structure inside, but it was very well done and set both the architectural style and the standard for almost the whole village centre, right down to present times. Most closely related to the

62 Ditton Park in the mid-19th century, by William Corden.

63 Skating on Ditton Park moat by William Corden, 1870s.

main house is the little 'Old Council Offices' building further east, see illustration 33, which was probably renovated by the same builder. On the other side of the Green the chemist's richly decorated façade, gables and shopfront incorporates many similar elements in work carried out rather later, probably around the turn of the century.

On the death of the Duchess of Buccleuch in 1895 there was a serious attempt to sell all the manorial property in Datchet and Ditton, which was by now superfluous to the main estate at Beaulieu. The Manor House range on the south side of The Green, with several shops and houses at the top of the High Street, was put up for auction in 1896 but they were not all sold until later. Ditton Park was heavily mortgaged by 1905 and was bought by the Admiralty Compass Department in 1917. In 1894 a new tenant leased Riding Court Farm from the Manor. John Kinross was one of the many farmers from Scotland who injected new expertise and enthusiasm into English farms, which had suffered during the agricultural depression of the previous decades. In 1912 the estate was sold to him outright and he ran

64 Manor House, 1912; on the right Manor Cottages (J. Dunster, draper, and C.J. Hunt, builders), on the left Cleversley builders. On extreme left, Old Council Offices with school belfry behind. Both the builders were also undertakers.

65 The drinking fountain given in 1886 by Lady Needham, with the chemist's shop and bank in a 1905 view.

66 John Kinross with his first wife and parents outside Riding Court, early 1900s. The agricultural trophies displayed are still in the family's possession.

67 John Kinross with tankard mangels in the orchard at Riding Court, about 1930.

68 Riding Court Dairy at 6 High Street (later Stevens' dairy), early 20th century.

it, partly as a market garden and dairy farm, until 1929. 'Jock' Kinross became a central figure in local life, behaving as, and treated as, the 'squire'. However, Lord Montagu remained Lord of Datchet Manor, and in 1961 he established the fact that although the Manor House had been sold to Mr. Killick, the 'Lordship' itself had not.

The Barker Bridge Trust; the Village Greens and Floods

Robert Barker's Bridge House Trust was responsible for creating our village greens, although the trustees could not have been aware at the outset how dramatic an effect their actions would have. Although there is no record of their decision to channel the village centre watercourse through a barrel-arched drain, the intention was probably to spend money effectively in a permanent solution, rather than to continue repairing the old road and foot bridges. They may also have been influenced by national concern over the dangers of stagnant water after the cholera outbreak of 1832. (Fear of the epidemic was great, but it was largely confined to the north of England and to London.) In April 1837 several new trustees were elected as the number had fallen to two, Isaac Gossett the vicar and John Richards the rector. Three farmers now joined them—John Goodwin and his son, and Robert Style who farmed Riding Court. These men had considerable knowledge and experience of farming and estate management, and would have been well aware of how to drain land and undertake major improvements. Their builder was a local man, Daniel Boulter, who lived in a cottage in London Road. He was first paid for work done in September 1837, just six months after the new trustees were elected, 'on account of the new arch built through the village'. Soon, all their funds were spent and only a loan of £100 from the vicar enabled the work to be finished.

Samuel Osborn wrote that the bricks for the culvert came from the wall built by William IV along the Windsor side of the river bank, a memory which, if true, would still have been current at the time he was writing. The first section of the or culvert was 182 feet long, three feet in diameter and with a barrel-shaped curve above and below the straight sides. It ran from roughly opposite the *Morning Star* to outside the village school, leaving quite a large pond at the foot of Slough Road and an open ditch at the eastern end. Ten years later, Daniel Boulter was again at work, 'building the arch or sewer to the end of the Road to Upton', taking it further west and filling in where the pond had been. In 1852, after complaints about offensive stagnant water at the other end of the sewer, the trustees decided to continue it to the east, to where it presently opens into the ditch across the new recreation ground.

Thus the Barker Bridge trustees had created the dry land of The Greens, without which it is almost impossible to imagine Datchet today. The ground was considered to belong to the Lord of the Manor, as did all land not specifically owned by anyone else. It was eventually given to the new Parish Council in 1895 by Lord Montagu, 'as open spaces, unbuilt on for ever, to be used for the purposes of a Village Green and recreation grounds'. The eastern section, called the Cut because its sides sloped down to the sunken culvert, had actually been given in 1881 by the Duke of Buccleuch as a recreation ground, but there was constant trouble caused by games played there so near to the road. The first known painting of the village was done in the 1860s by William Corden and shows the area of the Greens before they were grassed and railed in; it is earlier than the first photograph, which was taken in about 1875. Both William Cordens, the elder and the younger, lived at 6 High Street and were painters to the Royal family.

At the same time as all this expensive work was taking place, the Trust was fighting a losing battle against river floods. According to Osborn, the greatest floods in living memory were those of 1774, 1822, and 1828. In 1822 the corner of the *Horse and Groom* (the *Manor*

69 Village centre looking east, by William Corden, 1877. From right: *The Manor Hotel* before remodelling, Manor Cottages, the Manor House, builder's workshop, Old Council Offices and school bell tower behind. From left: new church steeple, Hall Cottage, Rose and Chestnut Cottages, blacksmith's workshop on corner.

70 First known photo of the village looking west, 1870s; from left, Manor House, Manor Cottages, *Manor Hotel* before remodelling, old *White Hart* building on High Street corner, *Morning Star* and Temple's building, then the blacksmith's, later Boots hardware.

71 'The Way to the Church', floods in Datchet in 1877 by William Corden. Although the pool was culverted by this date, the Greens frequently flooded and a temporary plank bridge was erected. From left, parish council shop (The Bridge), *The Royal Stag*, the rebuilt church, Hale and Pearce family blacksmith's workshop on the corner.

Hotel) was washed away by the force of the water. In time of flood, the Trust paid watchmen to observe the river banks all night, also providing beer and mending the lanterns. Sumptermead bank, still a feature of the golf course, was the village's main flood defence, and already of great age. A major repair had already been carried out in 1841, but in 1852 the trustees wrote to Henry Newman of The Willows, who occupied land and osier beds on the river bank: 'As the flood has risen to alarming height and as the emergency is very great and the danger of inundation of the village very imminent, I will thank you to do what is necessary to avert the overflow of water on to the roads and lands of the village'. This work eventually cost them £150, but in the 1870s there were again three serious floods in two years.

In 1883 the whole front page of *The Illustrated London News* depicted Datchet in full flood but in a humorous way. The drawing of the flooded common, 'a favourite haunt of Her Majesty's stag hounds', includes the only known illustration of Datchet mill, showing both the wind sails and the steam engine chimney. At the time of the next inundations, in 1891 and 1894, some excellent photographs were taken, which incidentally provide some of the best views of the village before the 20th century. From the 1870s fund raising events were held and collections made at times of flood, to help pay for coal to dry houses out and for lime to clean them, as well as to pay for rescue and supply operations.

The Trust also provided modern amenities for the village. From the 1860s they paid for oil lamps in the main streets and for fire hydrant

THE ILLUSTRATED LONDON NEWS

REGISTERED AT THE GENERAL POST-OFFICE FOR TRANSMISSION ABROAD.

No. 2288.—VOL. LXXXII.　　SATURDAY, FEBRUARY 24, 1883.　　WITH TWO SUPPLEMENTS | SIXPENCE. By Post, 6½D.

1. Datchet: a favourite drive of the Queen.
2. Datchet Common: a frequent meeting-place of her Majesty's Staghounds.
3. Datchet Station: "Walking the Plank."
4. Station at sea: sketched between Wraysbury and Datchet.
5. On the line near Wraysbury: a Sleeper Afloat.
6. The Theatre Train at Datchet Station: Fire versus Water.
7. Constabulary duty.
8. Going to the Train: High-street, Datchet.

72　*The Illustrated London News*, February 1883 (front cover): Floods in Datchet; at top right is 'Datchet Common, a frequent meeting place of Her Majesty's Staghounds', showing the sails and engine chimney of Datchet mill and Mill Place cottages.

73 Floods in 1891, looking towards *The Manor Hotel.*

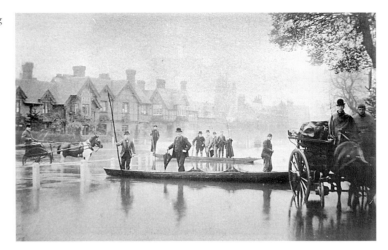

74 Floods in 1891, looking down Horton Road with the Working Men's Club in centre, grocer's shop on left corner.

75 Floods in 1894, with *The Royal Stag* and parish council shop on right; the third figure from right is Mr. Pearce, undertaker and descendant of the Hale family.

76 1891 or '94 floods; villagers gathered by the church gate at the edge of flood.

points when the water mains were laid in 1884. They contributed to the upkeep of the fire engine when in 1887 the Volunteer Brigade was started by Mr. Ward, and paid the rent of the shed by the station where the engine and the road watering cart were kept. Watering the roads was done in the summer to lay the dust, and there was a pump on the green for filling the carts. The Trust paid for the first public landing stage on the river front, built in 1865 by one of the Sears family.

The Coming of the Railway

Windsor was not one of the first towns served by the railway, and in fact there was considerable resistance to its arrival at all, from the Royal family, the Town Council, and Eton College. When agreement was reached in principle, both the Great Western and the London & South Western railway companies pressed forward branch lines. The G.W.R. made its approach from Slough, and the L. & S.W. from Richmond. Each had a problem in approaching Windsor; from Slough the line passing Eton was compelled to keep at a distance from the College, while from Datchet the only route was through Crown land. In 1849 the final stages developed into a race between the companies, narrowly won by the G.W.R., and resulted in Windsor's curious possession of two stations on different lines.

The line from Richmond was forced forward at a great pace from 1847, the company buying land at high prices along its course. The direct route lay through the very centre of Datchet and entailed the purchase of farm land and the sites of houses. The Goodwins were very well compensated for the loss of two old farmyards opposite each other in the High Street, one where the station is now, though Goodwyn House itself was skirted by a narrow margin. The Goodwins obtained a good bargain through their lawyers, but the Baptists considered themselves seriously injured by the proximity of the line to their new chapel. The presence of unruly navvies was felt to be a very real threat, and a letter expressing concern for the peace and morals of the inhabitants was sent to the company by the village.

The real problem came in obtaining permission for the line to cross the Home Park after having reached Black Potts on the parish boundary, where it abruptly terminated. The first train ran through Datchet on 22 August 1848. It caused great excitement, with large crowds dressed in their best clothes coming out at all the stations on the way to greet the eight carriages pulled by 'Centaur'. However, at a temporary station in Sumptermead field, now part of the golf course, passengers had to transfer to a coach and continue via Eton Road, either through Datchet and over the Thames by the old bridge to Windsor, or through Eton and over Windsor bridge.

The railway company was so desperate to reach Windsor that it was prepared to spend a huge amount of money in coming to an agreement with the Crown over the last section of the route. Prince Albert saw an opportunity of finally closing the public access through the castle grounds from Datchet and took a personal role in reaching a deal. In return for his allowing the rail line to cross the northern part of the Home Park, the L. & S.W.R. agreed to build a new road from Datchet riverside to Windsor, also crossing the Home Park, and two new bridges, the Victoria and the Albert, to carry it over the river to the north and south of Datchet. The original Thames bridge was then demolished, allowing the greater part of the Home Park to become completely private. The smaller section of the park beyond the road was given by the Crown for public use. All this work was rapidly completed, at the enormous cost of £60,000 and the Windsor Riverside station was opened in 1851. The last

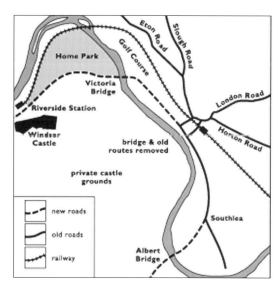

77 Plan of route changes brought about by the railway, *c.*1850.

78 High Street, looking south; the Baptist Chapel is right of centre. On the right corner is Hawes baker's shop, built in the 1880s to replace the old *White Hart* inn. In the distance, left of centre, by the level crossing, are three railway workers'cottages.

79   Turn-of-the-century traffic at the level crossing in the High Street.

80   A riverside regatta, 1907.

81 The Volunteer Review. Troops crossing the pontoon bridge at Datchet, from *The Illustrated London News*, 1868. The 218ft. span was erected in 28 minutes.

drawing of Datchet bridge, just before its demolition, shows the *Crown and Angel* advertising, 'Good Stabling, Two Minutes from Datchet Station', thus recording the brief moment when the ancient river crossing point met the future in the shape of the railway age, and also its final demise. Perhaps the most famous person known to have used Datchet station was Charles Dickens, who varied his routes to Slough where his mistress Ellen Tiernan lived, often walking there from Datchet or Windsor to maintain secrecy.[1]

By 1850 the national development of railways had greatly reduced the volume of goods being transported by river and for several decades the upper reaches of the Thames were largely left to the fishermen. Then from the

1880s people began to flock out of London in huge numbers by train for pleasure trips on the river, and especially to the fashionable Henley Regatta, where the social whirl mattered rather more than the actual racing. While the other main centres of this new tourist trade were Reading, Maidenhead and Windsor, Datchet had its share of summer visitors. At first it was the fishermen who hired out punts; the well known George Keene, who lived at Thames Cottage in the High Street, was one of the first in the area to do so. Martha Cox was listed as a boat proprietor in 1887, at an ancient barn in Back Lane (now Queen's Road), and by 1891 Fenn's boatyard was established on the old wharf site at the riverfront. There was even a Datchet

Regatta, a minor affair compared with Henley, and described in 1888 thus:

> Well, we did nothing but eat, drink, and laugh. I believe a good many of the village boys won small sums of money. I think a good many gentlemen showed considerable ignorance of punting, and I know that there was much good natured chaff and not a few wet skins over the dongola [*sic*] and canoe races. Though a good many people sneered at the 'Regatta' it was excellent fun all the same, and after all why shouldn't a few generous gentlemen provide Datchet with a yearly water-party. Certainly the houseboat illuminations were quite as good as Henley, and the fireworks. I dare say a hundred house-boats followed down the stream to the Ellis's lovely house [Rosenau], where the whole grounds and those of Mrs. Fowler's next door [Sandlea House] were blazing a thousand lamps. Then we had more fireworks, more cheering for the genial Mr. Ellis, and so to bed.[2]

Jerome K. Jerome's *Three Men in a Boat*, published in 1889, also describes Datchet as a minor riverside resort. Although Jerome paints a comic and fictional picture of the village and the difficulty of finding hotel beds, he does introduce the real *Manor Hotel* and *Stag*, with the grocer's next door to it, into his story. Between the 1860s and 1880s the memory of the old bridge was revived several times by the building of pontoon bridges across the river on the original site. These bridges were built as military exercises during volunteer troop reviews and by the regulars during visits of the Shah of Persia and the Viceroy of Egypt. Once again, people could walk across the temporary bridges to the review grounds in the Home Park opposite.

The Rebuilding of The Church

In 1853 a new vicar replaced Isaac Gossett, who had been in the post since 1814. The Rev. Henry Francis Udney Hall almost immediately set about raising funds to rebuild the church completely. Victorian religious revival and reform, leading to new churches being built and others being brought up to date, was at its peak around 1850. Several contemporary drawings show that Datchet's church was in a fairly disgraceful condition, and it was also considered too small for the growing population. A census of church attendance taken in 1851 found an average congregation of 240 people, with seats for 367, but provision was officially required for 58 per cent of the population. The church therefore needed to be enlarged to provide seating for 530 people. From the outset, it was also planned to pull down the old vicarage to the north of the church and build a new one much further north, to allow the church-yard to be extended because it was very nearly full. The Duke of Buccleuch had offered to provide a completely new site for a church and burial ground elsewhere in the parish, but when this was rejected he offered £150 to the restoration fund instead. Similar large sums were promised by the dean and canons of St George's and Queen Victoria, and by the wealthiest inhabitants. Within a few years, all households of any social standing had contributed, some as little as one shilling, and the subscription list was made public. Raphael Brandon, a minor Gothic Revival architect, was engaged, but it soon became clear that sufficient money could not be raised from the village to carry out the whole rebuilding at once.

Eventually, the work was completed piecemeal in three stages which took more than a decade, from 1857 to 1869. The most necessary work was done in the first phase, the restoration of the chancel and the rebuilding of the nave. The chancel is the only part of the building still retaining its medieval size and shape, though probably little of the original material survives, and the stone tracery of its old east window was replaced by a copy. The length of the nave was restricted by the site, but a wide new south aisle helped provide more space. The present south porch was added, and also a new vestry projecting north from the chancel. All this was done between May and December 1857, during which time church services were held in the village school.

The second phase then began, with the demolition of the vicarage house and the building of its grand replacement much further north. It was designed by the same architect and built by the same contractors, Dove Brothers, as was the church. The church and burial ground could then be extended by using the site of the old vicarage and some of its garden. The new tower was built over the east end of the new north aisle, an odd construction in which the five bells could not be safely swung, and Thomas Hammerson the blacksmith made a frame by which the bells could be struck instead. At this stage, the work could have been considered complete, as 529 seats were provided in new pews, but in 1864 a vestry meeting decided that the building was still too small, 'especially for the families of working men'.

82 'The Church at Datchet in its present state' 1852, viewed from the north east.

83 Interior of the church before rebuilding, by William Corden, 1857. Looking into the chancel, the Wheeler wall monuments can just be seen. Above the chancel are boards giving texts of the Lord's Prayer, Ten Commandments and other scriptures. On the left within the aisle is a private curtained pew, and on the right a gallery where the poor would have sat. A similar gallery ran across the west end for musicians.

Another motive may be suspected here, that of removing these families beyond contact with rich and respectable inhabitants. In the old church, there was a gallery over the south aisle to which the poor would probably have been consigned, as well as a west gallery where the musicians played. Now two new areas well removed from the main body of the church were created, an outer north aisle, and an extension of the nave to the west, which was made possible by encroaching on Bridge Trust property behind the *Royal Stag*. At the same time, room was made for a modern organ, paid for by the vicar, in an extension of the south aisle alongside the chancel.

Work stopped at last in 1869, having produced a fashionable church in a deliberately plain Early English revival style, but unconventional in its plan. Many of the original memorials were re-sited and a different opportunity for commemorating the dead was provided by the new windows. These are the most striking feature of the church, most of the stained glass being by one company, O'Connor of London, and several of the windows were dedicated by the parishioners to Prince Albert who had died in 1861. The artist William Corden recorded the church, both its interior and exterior, in paintings deliberately done before and after the rebuilding.

However, the churchyard problem had only been temporarily solved. By the 1890s it was again almost full and a new cemetery was necessary. The Dowager Duchess of Buccleuch gave a plot of land in Ditton Road and Mrs. Crake, of the Lawn, offered to build a chapel at her own expense but under a strict condition: no services were to take place there except those of the Church of England. When the cemetery became the responsibility of the new Parish Council in 1896, she had an inscription recording this stipulation placed on a wall of the chapel. Recently, this caused problems which contributed to the abandonment of the chapel for burial services. The building is particularly interesting for its stained glass windows, including one by Morris & Co. The Baptist Chapel had been built in 1841 on the site of the old stable or barn which was first registered as their meeting house in 1795. It had tall gothic windows along the side facing the High Street and a small one in the gable end. The arrival of the railway so near was a great blow, but the chapel continued in use for more than another hundred years.

84 St Mary's Church from London Road after the rebuilding, by William Corden.

85   High Street looking north in 1914. The windows on the left are those of the Baptist Chapel built in 1841. Next along is the house built by the Lord of the Manor in the mid-18th century, now 6 & 8 High Street.

The Founding of the School

There were several schools in Datchet by 1830, but they were mostly private day or boarding establishments for young ladies. One was at Cedar House, one in part of the Lawn, and by 1840 there was another at Clifton House and The Cottage in the High Street. A school of some sort was also run by the church, as in 1817 Isaac Gossett advertised in the *Windsor Express* for 'A steady woman capable of instructing children in Reading, Working [i.e. needlework] and Knitting'. Parochial day schools offering this sort of teaching are known to have been held in the Manor House building and in an old cottage on the site of the modern Bank House. However,

things were changing and the need for elementary education of the poor was being recognised by Parliament.

In 1841 an Act of Parliament was passed which encouraged landowners to grant sites for such schools. The timing suggests that Lord Montagu and his nephew, the 5th Duke of Buccleuch, were responding to this in 1843, when the village school was founded. The land they gave adjoined the Manor House range, where a schoolroom and schoolmistress's house were built by public subscription. The school was never affiliated to the Church of England's National Society for Promoting the Education of the Poor, although it was often referred to later as the National School. It was certainly run by the parish church, as the land grant of 1844 specifies:

> ... such school to be under the management, control and inspection of the Vicar of the Parish, to be used for the purposes of educating the children of poor persons of the Parish according to the Principles of the Established Church of England, and for no other purpose.

The personal intervention of Henry James, Lord Montagu may be suspected here, as he was implacably opposed to any dissent from the established church. At Beaulieu, he was able to threaten eviction from estate dwellings if they were used for education other than Church of England instruction of children; saying that there were other schools 'of that nature on the outskirts of the parish, of which parents could avail themselves'. In Datchet the Lord of the Manor had much less control over people's religious freedom as there were so few estate cottages.

The school's written records begin in 1862, when the first of its extensions was built to cope with the rising population and to accommodate older children as well as infants. From then on, every decade saw further enlargements to the south, each requiring a new grant of manorial land until the site extended almost to the railway line. When a large new room was built in 1897 the devastating floods of 1891 and 1894 were fresh in the village's memory and it was deliberately built at a higher level up several steps, safe from the inevitable floods in the future. From 1862 to 1900 Mr. and Mrs. Huntley ran the school and lived in the school house with their own children. He was in charge of the Upper School for children from age seven to about twelve, while she was the Governess for

86   The village school in about 1912. The spire was on top of the bell tower; the original bell now hangs in the school hall. The group of three chimneys served the fireplaces in the original schoolroom and the adjoining teacher's house.

87   Infants' class, 1915; this room is still in use, though it has been remodelled many times.

the infants. The school was regularly inspected by both Government and Diocesan inspectors and for most of the period had a good reputation. But in his later years Mr. Huntley became very deaf and the Inspector complained of '... the continual buzz of conversation, which in so large a school is a serious blot, the children take advantage of Mr. Huntley being unable to hear it'. The oldest living memory confirms this, recalling that he used an ear trumpet and Iadministered thrashings on the basis of his skill in lip reading. From 1870 the local school attendance board waged a long battle against absence due to working in the fields, to bad weather, poor health, and to better attractions elsewhere, such as a local circus, rabbit coursing on the common, or the soldiers marching between London and Windsor. An annual School Treat was provided for the children, consisting of sports, games, sweets, and tea in the grounds of one of the many grand houses, after an obligatory church service.

Many other philanthropic works and entertainments were enthusiastically organised by the ladies of the parish for the adults as well as the children of deserving lower classes. A Nursing Society provided medical help for the needy sick, and Sunday Schools were run in the schoolrooms, with an annual tea and a Christmas tree. Men and boys could attend gardening, allotment cultivation, technical, or carving classes. There were also classes for decorative arts and needlework, which culminated in exhibitions inspected by the Queen and her daughters who bought some of the work. The prizes given on these occasions show how distinct the social classes were; those for plain needlework discriminating between 'cottagers' and 'women in domestic employment', while 'honorary exhibits' were contributed by wealthy and titled ladies for admiration only. The Prince Consort's Association, founded to encourage a variety of domestic and technical arts and crafts, also gave

88   Schoolgirls in their playground on the west side of the school, about 1912.

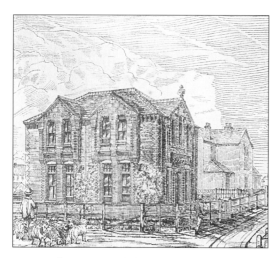

89 Working Men's Club, opened by HRH Princess Christian in 1881; the porch was added for Queen Victoria's Golden Jubilee in 1887. On the left are the cottages in Green Lane, now mostly rebuilt. A fenced path leads to the Tarrant's farmhouse, built after 1875 on former Goodwin land.

prizes for 'Bringing up a Family', and for 'Keeping a Clean Cottage'. These, which seem so patronising to a modern view, were then part of the accepted social order, demonstrated also by the poor people's pride in 'having six Sirs in our village'.

Many of these classes, exhibitions and concerts were held in the new Working Men's Club, built in 1881 on another plot of land given by the Lord of the Manor, though it was begun in 1878 as a social club by George Cleversley at the old workhouse building in Holmlea Road. It was intended to provide an alternative to the ubiquitous public house in an attempt to raise moral and educational standards. With a further room built at the back and paid for by Lady Needham, it also functioned as the first village hall. Social life at all levels was flourishing, and many of our own institutions, clubs and societies had their origins in Victorian times. The golf club was founded in 1895, and children were recruited from the school to act as caddies, while the history of the cricket club goes back even further to 1869 when their first game was recorded. Later, there was also a football team which played games on Gillett's back meadow, the site of the present Linchfield Road.

The Growth of the Population and New Houses

Population figures from the beginning of the 19th century show a slow growth from about 700 in 1811 to 990 in 1871. After that the rise was much steeper, reaching 2,050 by 1911, with the greatest increase occurring in the 1880s. While the impact of the railway's arrival was not immediate, Datchet's expansion during this period was due to the railway opening up the village as a dormitory suburb of London as well as a satellite of Windsor, which it had always been. As ever, the river played its part. In 1875 all the Goodwin property was sold after a dispute about inheritance. The auction catalogue, encouraging the buying of land for housing development, stated, 'The difficulties of obtaining houses in Datchet are increasing with the growing passion for riverside enjoyment', and desirable new residences were built on many of the plots bought at that sale. In the past there had been grand families of independent means and wealthy farmers, but from the 1870s new middle-class and professional occupations appear; bankers, stock-brokers, barristers, surgeons, and merchants trading across the Empire.

As the building boom developed, Datchet swarmed with bricklayers, painters, decorators and plumbers, as well as blacksmiths and wheel-wrights, many of them local men adapting to new opportunities as their traditional agricultural work became mechanised. In 1841, there were 95 agricultural labourers in a population of 922, but in 1871 this had reduced to 55 in a total of 980. Many men who had previously worked in the fields seem to have become private coachmen, grooms and gardeners at the new grand houses and villas, although market gardening was also flourishing. The railway itself offered employment to some, but the skilled engineering jobs were done by newcomers from the Midlands, the North and from Wales. In the later censuses a great many women are recorded as working, and they may well have been doing so earlier, although the information was not asked for. The poorest worked as laundresses, many of the more respectable were dressmakers, and several ran beerhouses or shops. Some women also headed family businesses after the death of their husbands, including Thirza Bidwell, who ran a plumbing firm at the present Old Manor House, and Elizabeth Pearce at the Church Cottage smithy. There were shops and craftsmen supplying the everyday needs of the ordinary people; butchers, grocers, bakers, dairymen, drapers, shoemakers, tailors and sweet shops, but never the wider range of shops that would be found in a town.

At the beginning of this period, the cottages rented by the poor were wretched, and none have survived into the present. There were too few of them so they were over-crowded, and little responsibility was felt by their owners to keep them fit for habitation. The old workhouse was still lived in as separate apartments, with an added cottage block in the grounds, and there were little rows of tenements on the common and at the far end of Slough Road, so that as much as possible the poor were both out of sight and out of mind. One slum row did survive into this century, called Challoner Row and running behind Astracot. This terrace of nine timber-framed tenements had overhanging upper storeys which suggests that they were very old indeed. Each had two tiny rooms down and two up and were without access to clean water or drainage. Diseases which frequently killed children—diphtheria, scarlet fever and the dreaded smallpox—were particularly rife in conditions like these where the nine households could have more than thirty children altogether, concentrated in a space which is now a small garden.

Some of the first decent working-class houses were built in about 1850 for their employees by the railway company on land adjacent to the line and station. Rather later, much more development of this type took place on 'the Common', in Horton Road, Holmlea Road, at the foot of Ditton Road, Penn Road and New Road. The Sears family, who were in business as bricklayers with the Boulters by 1860, expanded into buying land and built many of these new houses on the Common. With its solidly working- and artisan-class population, its own shops, blacksmiths and beerhouses, Datchet Common became virtually a separate community at the eastern end of Datchet. Its oldest beerhouse was the *Plough*, with the *Harrow* round the corner towards the old workhouse, and later the *Rising Sun* which dates from around 1870. In order to encourage people to attend the Church of England, services were held regularly at the Cemetery Chapel which was nearer the Common than the parish church. In 1891 there was also a Wesleyan Mission Room in Woodbine Cottages near the *Rising Sun*, but it does not seem to have become established as a chapel.

Several of the terrace rows and pairs of houses still bear their Victorian names: Jubilee, Albert and Victoria Cottages. At the top of Mill Place is a group of cottages which are older than they look, built about 1860 on his own land by George Jaques the miller. The mill continued in use into the 1880s, when it was driven by a steam engine. The windmill, the chimney and the cottages can all be seen in an *Illustrated London News* front-page drawing of 1883. In the 1880s, workmen's cottages were also built much nearer the village in Green Lane, although all except a few in Datchet Place and Percy Place have been replaced in recent times. None of these developments were council housing, but built speculatively by those who either owned the land or had capital to invest in houses built to rent out, often local farmers, builders, or successful tradesmen.

The rich and the aspiring lived elsewhere, and in a grand fashion. Among the earliest of the new Victorian houses was the White Lodge pair on Southlea Road, built before 1870 in an Italianate style on one of the first enclosure plots to be sold for building. The land bought by the railway was some of the first to be opened up to completely new developments in the 1880s, along the Avenue down towards the river, and then into Montagu Road. At the end of the Avenue, Dr. Samuel Osborn built The Maisonette, and the gold bullion dealer

90 Accident at the *Plough*, Horton Road, 1905. A tree fell through the roof and Cleversley the builder is in attendance.

91 1947 floods, Army DUKW in Horton Road, looking east.

Benjamin Elkin Mocatta built Leyfield (now Swancourt), both taking advantage of their prime corner sites facing the river, and both in a revival mock-timbered style. Further down Southlea Road is the huge Riverbank, built in the grand late Victorian manner for Sir William Shipley, Mayor of Windsor. The Shipley family also built a much more restrained house, now demolished, called the Hall in the centre of the village on the site of the Goodwins' old College Farm. In the adjacent plot, facing the Green, a grand pair of semi-detached villas, now Patrixbourne and North Green, appear to echo the gables and mock timbering of the Manor House, but with an extravagant little turret at the corner. Nearby is the enormous stone-faced Ormonde, quite out of character with the rest of the village, which William Dove built after his work on the church. It was at first occupied as a boys' boarding school or religious seminary.

Buccleuch Road was newly laid out on the old Pound Close, bought from the Lord of the Manor in 1888, where there had been no previous building due to the threat of flooding. Development along the marshy area of Slough Road was delayed until about 1890 for the same reason. The most interesting of the houses there is Moy Lodge which is in the style of a Malaysian tea planter's bungalow, and was actually built by a tea merchant returning from the far east. Sir William Good's Churchmead House was approached from the Slough Road but stood well back on land which had belonged to John Richards, surrounded by an old plantation of trees. It was pulled down after the war and Churchmead School has been built in its grounds.

Nearly all of these were new developments, but in Horton Road the old high status properties also attracted attention. In 1850 Sir John Crake bought the Lawn from the Manor, into whose hands it had fallen for want of a purchaser, and it was sold on condition that a full renovation would take place. By the 1860s all the old houses and cottages surrounding the

92   Leyfield, now Swancourt, in 1905, built for the Mocatta family on The Avenue corner, facing the river.

93   The Hall (right), built on the old Goodwin's farm site by the Shipley family, and Patrixbourne, built at the turn of the century. In the centre stands the 1897 Jubilee Cross.

main house had been demolished to clear the way for garden grounds, with a new group of model cottages built on the western edge of the estate. The same process was carried out at the old Canister House property, which was bought from the Earley family by Sir John Gore in the 1820s. He was a Vice Admiral who served under Nelson and died in Datchet a year after the loss of his only son from his own ship. By 1840 Lord Howick had built Leigh House in its place, which was sold several times to other titled owners until it became the home of the Ladies Cholmondeley in around 1890. One of the old Lascelles family farmsteads was obliterated with the formation of its large private grounds, and a new lodge was built by the entrance drive opening into London Road. The nearby Cedar and Satis Houses did survive, but by the end of the century almost the whole of the once densely built-up Horton Road area was temporarily swallowed up by these two great estates. At Southlea, the two old riverside houses, Rosenau and Sandlea, were bought by the Commissioners for Woods and Forests to complete the control exercised by the Crown over land opposite the private Home Park. (Paul Mellon, the American millionaire, spent a summer at Sandlea in 1904.) By the end of the century the Commissioners had also bought Southlea Farm and the house just south of it, which may originally have belonged to the Barker family. This house, which has since burned down, was occupied by Sir Henry Simpson, veterinary surgeon to the Queen, and the farm buildings were converted to stalls for over seventy horses.

The Jubilees and the Turn of the Century

The first of the monuments to be built on the new Greens was the drinking fountain. In 1886 it was presented to the village by Lady Georgiana Needham of Datchet House, then in her 90th year (all her sisters lived to similar great ages). The fountain provided water for humans, dogs, and horses in three separate bowls. The water supply was paid for by the Barker Bridge Trust, as was the electric lamp at its pinnacle. But it was also designed to supply something just as important, the succour of the spirit of those who drank. Biblical texts referring to the water of life are carved in its pink Aberdeen granite on all sides. Such a public demonstration of piety accompanying practical good works was typical of the time, and also perpetuated the name of its benefactor in the village where she was socially beneath only the Duchess of Buccleuch and the Queen herself.

The Queen's Golden Jubilee in 1887 was marked by the planting of an oak tree from the Duchess's Ditton Park. The schoolchildren planted it after a church service, in a gaily decorated village ringing to the sound of 'God Save The Queen'. A great party was held in Ditton Park for the whole village, culminating in a visit from the Queen who drove around the assembled crowds in her carriage at the end of the day. Her Diamond Jubilee was commemorated by a village cross presented by Mrs. Crake, who unveiled it herself. There was originally a plaque recording both her gift and her 70 years as a parishioner in Datchet, but only the one dedicating the monument to Queen Victoria has survived. The Queen did not visit the village on this occasion, but all the children went to the Home Park for their Jubilee party, together with 6,000 others from around Windsor. Mrs. Rawlings, who in 1999 was 107 years old, remembers walking to the park and seeing Queen Victoria driving round the great circle of children, sitting bolt upright and looking straight ahead rather than towards the crowds. Being so near to Windsor itself, the village events for both Jubilees paled into insignificance beside celebrations in the town; for a week there were decorations, fireworks, bands, processions and enormous crowds, on a wave of patriotism and an unprecedented scale which has perhaps seldom been equalled since.

But the end of the period was already signalled; great changes were on their way. Local government in the shape of Datchet Parish

94   The 1897 Jubilee Cross, with the Jubilee oak tree (*centre*) and drinking fountain (*on left*), looking towards the *Manor Hotel* in an early 1900s postcard.

Council was established in 1894, as in all rural areas. There was great reluctance to relinquish the traditional power of the parish church in Datchet, as the new democratic councils took over many of the secular responsibilities which until then had been managed by the church's vestry meetings. Election of the council was delayed until as late as possible in the year, and there was an immediate dispute requiring a second election two weeks later. For the first time, the vicar was not automatically in charge of village meetings, and awkward questions were soon being asked by those who had come into office. During the past century, the Barker Bridge Trust had gradually, although not deliberately, come under the control of the clergy rather than of laymen, and now its position was queried; was it a church or a parish charity? The Trust's role was made more difficult as so many of its functions (road watering, lighting, flood banks), were now to be the responsibility of the new council, though the trustees continued to provide much of the funding. The status of the old almshouse (since 1820 rented out as a shop), the poor's land and other charities were also questioned by a strong anti-church faction. There were no easy answers to the questions and serious disputes often occurred, including personal threats. Satisfactory solutions to many issues were not finalised for another fifty years or more, and problems from the past still surface even now.

The First Car and the First Aeroplane

At almost the same time, in 1895, a remarkable harbinger of the future arrived in Datchet. The Hon. Evelyn Ellis, who lived at Rosenau, one of the old riverside houses at Southlea, was keenly aware of the development of the motor car on the continent and foresaw its possibilities. In England self-propelled vehicles were under the constraint of the red flag law, designed to restrict the speed of traction engines on public roads, but applied to all other horseless vehicles. Ellis deliberately flouted the law by importing from France the first motor car in England, and driving it from Micheldever in Hampshire to his home in Datchet. His Panhard-Levassour, still preserved in the Science Museum, was instrumental in gaining the repeal of the act, and with his associates he can be considered to have helped to found the motor industry in this country. Ellis's horseless carriage was a great curiosity, visited by many who were treated to a drive at exciting speeds of up to 20 miles an hour. John Scott Montagu of Ditton Park must have known of Ellis's motor car and owned one himself a year or two later, starting his family's pioneering interests. Between 1911 and 1914, cars were actually made in Datchet in the Talbot's Home Farm workshops near the site of the old workhouse in Holmlea Road, where Lord Montagu was the landlord. The firm G.W.K. (Grice, Wood and Keiller) made a light car there, using an early application of friction transmission, and winning race medals at Brooklands and on the London to Edinburgh run in 1912. K.L.G. sparking plugs were also made at the works until the firm removed to Maidenhead in 1914.

One more ingredient of modern times, the aeroplane, arrived in Datchet in 1911. As a young dare devil, Tommy Sopwith had raced motor bikes around the village greens when staying with his mother who rented one half of the Manor House from Lord Montagu. By 1910 he had learned to fly at Brooklands and was soon winning prizes for pioneering flights in British-made machines. In January 1911, when he landed here on the golf course, few people had ever seen a plane before and around a thousand villagers rushed out to see it, while Tommy went into the *Manor Hotel* for a cup of coffee. Mr. Page, who had become headmaster of the village school in 1900, wrote an article in the *Windsor and Eton Express*, describing the day thus:

> Seated on Sunday afternoon, enjoying my usual rest, I was suddenly awakened by someone violently ringing the bell. On opening the door my visitor in gasping breath exclaimed: 'An aeroplane! An aeroplane! Mr. Sopwith has alighted on the golf links

95 The Hon. Evelyn Ellis and his 1895 Panhard-Levassour at Rosenau.

96 Tommy Sopwith, later Sir Thomas, in about 1911.

and is returning very shortly'. The fields and roads seemed alive with people, and never before have I seen such a gathering on the golf course. I came at last to the now-to-be-famous spot, and found the bird machine quietly resting. Almost at once the intrepid aviator took his seat and awe and wonder pervaded the field. Such was the solemn stillness that one could hear the ticking of a watch. 'See', said one, 'The engine is starting'. Instantly, the motor buzzed, the forward plane was elevated and the aeroplane ran along on its wheels for about 150 yards, when it began to mount into the air. Returning, it ascended higher and no words could describe the gracefulness of its movement and the excitement of the occasion. 'It seems a dream', said one, whilst another could hardly believe his eyes when the airship sped away from sight amidst the applause of the onlookers. The youth of the aviator, the placidity of his countenance as he manoeuvred his machine and the charm of his smile electrified the crowd. Those fortunate enough to have been present went home to relate for many a day, and to remember for their allotted span, the first descent of the epoch-making aeroplane on the golf links of Datchet.[3]

Tom Sopwith returned two weeks later for a demonstration in front of the King at Windsor, using the golf course as his take off point for the East Lawn of the Castle and circling the Round Tower on his way. Afterwards, the plane was left at Datchet overnight because of fog and Mr. Page gave all the schoolchildren time off to go and see it. Little did he know how familiar a sight that plane's successors were going to be to those very children.

But, for the time being, cars and planes were only occasional novelties; the horse was still paramount. Children particularly looked forward to Ascot races, when the post horns would sound at Ditton corner and they would gather to see the coaches drive down London Road. Little boys turned cartwheels, calling 'Good luck!' and 'Throw out your mouldy coppers', in the hope of being thrown pennies, but both adults and children bowed or curtseyed when King George and Queen Mary came past. Pennies were also to be earned at the Windsor Guard's polo ground in Horton Road by holding the horses, and many followed them with a shovel to collect manure for the garden. When a band accompanied the guards, children knew that the Prince of Wales was on his way to play polo there. Lady Bowes-Lyon, a relation of our Queen Mother, lived at Horton and would come to Datchet to shop in her bucket cart, drawn by a pony which drank from the fountain in the village. This time is remembered as a golden age by the oldest villagers, when they watched the reapers and gleaned in the fields after harvest, getting into trouble with Jock Kinross for making houses in the stooks of corn.

Chapter Six

Change and Continuity:
From 1914 to the Present

The first half of the 20th century is characterised by the two wars which resulted in greater government intervention in local affairs everywhere, and the second half by recovery, prosperity and growth which has brought new problems yet to be solved.

The First World War

In all communities, the greatest impact of this war was the terrible slaughter of its young men. Compared with the 1939-45 war, those at home suffered fewer privations and they were also unaware until afterwards of how appalling conditions at the front actually were. There are villagers who still remember seeing the glow in the sky during air raids on London, and a Zeppelin over Windsor, but, unknown to most people at the time, vital secret war work was being carried out at Ditton Park. The Admiralty Compass Observatory, which had bought the secluded house and grounds from Lord Montagu in 1917, tested all the compasses produced for both ships and aircraft during the war, the work mainly being done by women. Navigational training for pilots was also carried out there, and research into more sophisticated navigation aids.

One of the first reactions at home was fund raising, which became more desperate as the war developed. By 1915 there were several families of Belgian refugees in Datchet who were provided with lodgings, food, clothing and coal from collecting boxes around the village and by the schoolchildren's pennies, there being no state benefits to support them. Lady Cholmondeley accepted two of these families into Leigh House. There were also units of Territorials billeted in the village and the school was used as a recreation centre for them in the evenings, with ladies providing refreshments. Lady Marcia de Paravicini of Riverside House set up a collection point for eggs for wounded soldiers, to be sent to hospitals including King Edward VII in Windsor, her total being 11,001 eggs. Special collections of money and goods were made to send parcels of Christmas comforts to troops abroad and to prisoners of war.

Gradually, many village activities and institutions became affected by the absence of men and the need for women to take on war work. This had a very significant impact on the changing role of women and contributed to their gaining the right to vote. The Mothers' Meetings were abandoned as its leaders, Mrs. Batty and Mrs. Fletcher, went to work in hospitals for the wounded, and women ran Datchet's War Supply depot, collecting household linen and almost anything re-usable. The Girls' Friendly Society spent their time knitting socks, gloves and scarves as a patriotic duty, while the Boy Scouts won War Service badges by assisting the local police. Mrs. Harvey, the vicar's wife, gave lectures for women on

Household Economy and Cooking in War-time, and an Infant Welfare Centre was opened for the first time. Men too old or young for service abroad joined the Voluntary Service Corps, making themselves proficient in drill and shooting. The Horticultural Society found a new and important role in encouraging the growing of vegetables and keeping of poultry, so their annual show did continue, but without tents or bands. The daylight saving scheme introduced 'summer time' in 1915 which was a confusing novelty, but not as disruptive as the government's taking over of the railways in 1914, which caused normal timetables to be abandoned.

The toll of deaths at the front was greatest from the Common end of the village, since the population of young working men was concentrated there, though officer sons of the Kinross and de Paravicini families were also killed, causing great shock in the village as they were such prominent figures. The Carrod, Newens, Widcombe and Johnson families all lost two sons, though one of the saddest deaths

was that of James Hale Pearce, grandson of the Hale family. He was in hospital in France after being gassed, and his parents were rushed over to see him, as was his dying wish, but they arrived too late.

In all, 54 men did not return, and in 1919 village meetings began to consider what form a memorial to them should take, a topic being discussed in every other village and town in the country. The first ideas, apart from a monument, included a Victory Hall, endowed beds at Edward VII hospital, or an almshouse for the elderly. But the earliest memorial to be erected, and now almost completely forgotten, was the crucifix at the entrance to the village in London Road, which was given by the Curling family. It was intended as a wayside shrine, familiar to those who had served in France but unusual in England, and was dedicated in May 1919 by the Bishop of Buckingham after a full procession from the church. The second was the Celtic cross just inside the churchyard gate, described as the women's memorial, and eventually there was

97   Soldiers on 'Cleversley's bridge' across the floods in 1915.

98 The Lord Lieutenant of Buckinghamshire unveiling the War Memorial, 1920. Behind, to the left, is the house and builders' workshops which had belonged to the Sears, Boulters, Bidwells and then Cleversleys, on the site of the present WI hall and its two shops.

also a Roll of Honour in the church itself. The monument on the Green was designed by Lionel Cust of Datchet House and paid for by collections from all social classes in the village. It was unveiled in May 1920 by the Lord Lieutenant of Buckinghamshire, who was introduced to the crowds by John Kinross of Riding Court in a long and moving speech. As well as the names of the fallen, the numbers of those who had served both abroad and at home were given, even down to those who had worked at the hospital supply depot, and John Kinross said that it was only want of space that prevented all these names being recorded individually, as the committee would have liked.

The family of Lionel, later Sir Lionel, Cust was related through a cousin to the Needham family, who had previously lived in Datchet House. He was an art historian of considerable reputation, keeper of the National Portrait Gallery and surveyor of the king's pictures. He became a close friend of Edward VII and wrote a book on the King and his court, to which he belonged as a gentleman usher, and a history of Eton College. It is to his lifelong work in the arts that we owe the fine design of the 1920 obelisk, carved with military arms and pictorial scenes as well as the names of the dead and the numbers of those who had served at home and abroad. Sir Lionel was also extremely active in the church and many other parish organisations, and it was said that he had a gift for enjoying simple pleasures.

The 1920s and 1930s

During the war, great changes had taken place in government organisation and administration, forced by the need to manage food supply and transport and control industry to produce munitions. The result by the end of the war was a much more interventionist policy in social matters, so that the war years mark a more significant change, even in rural areas, than did the end of the Victorian era. From 1919 a series of Housing Acts required that local authorities should survey the housing needs in their areas and submit plans for new provision from State funds—the emergence of council housing. By 1919 it was noted that all the houses and cottages in the village were occupied, a very unusual situation and indicative of the shortage which was recognised nationally. John Kinross considered that 12 more cottages were needed in Datchet to house the number of people engaged in agriculture, and the Parish Council decided to report to Eton Rural District Council that 30 more should be built, to ease severe overcrowding and to cater for the families of men returning from the front.

99   Queen Mary with Mrs. Susan Lewin on a visit to the allotment cottages in Ditton Road, 1919.

However, before any council houses were provided, the first modern cottages in Datchet were built next to the cemetery in Ditton Road by the Datchet Co-Partnership Housing and Allotment Society, the first such society in the country, which was started by Mr. Ward. The chairman of the society was Lionel Cust, who in 1919 brought the King and Queen on an unannounced visit to the cottages, which they thoroughly inspected both inside and out. A delightful photograph was taken of Mrs. Lewin, still in her working apron, shyly talking to the Queen about her 14 children and especially the five sons who had returned from the war.

At the same time, awareness of the huge numbers of children in work brought about a new Education Act which raised the school leaving age to fourteen. This caused enormous pressure on the village school, but for the first time free secondary education was available for the most able children, and the whole school had a half holiday to celebrate the first grammar school place won by Winifred Avis in 1920. Rose Mash won a place at the same time, but was unable to accept the offer as her family could not afford the associated costs. For the new senior children staying on at school, there was practical work in gardening for the boys and shorthand classes for the girls, who also went to Langley once a week for domestic science. The war had delayed much needed work on the school buildings, and the pressure of older children brought matters to a head. The school was threatened with immediate closure and rebuilding as a state rather than as a church school unless £5,000 could be raised in order to comply with the new standards being set, mainly in matters of health, hygiene and smaller classes. Frantic fund raising took place, as the church was determined not to relinquish its role in education. Donations were sought from far afield, and one reply to the vicar's plea expressed surprise that Datchet could have any trouble in finding the money as it appeared such a well-off village. The vicar answered that such a view was a superficial

100   Children and nannies on the riverfront, 1929.

impression and that away from the village centre there was a great deal of poverty and poor living conditions. The target was finally reached and a complete remodelling of the Victorian school took place in 1926. Much of the credit for surviving this terrible period must go to E.W. Page, known to the children as 'Gaffer', who took over the headship from Mr. Huntley in 1900. However, he retired during the building work and it was Mr. Hawkins who took charge of the greatly improved school. Mr. Page continued to serve as a school governor and on the parish council, writing excellent booklets on the history of the village and publishing detailed research into the background of the Barker Bridge Trust and the charities for the poor, in all of which he was involved.

Village traditions were clearly topical at this time, as in 1925 the bounds were beaten for the first time since 1904, as a deliberate revival of an old custom which in itself no longer had any real meaning. The event was given a modern significance by the vicar, Rev. Russell Potter, at a service to start the day, when he said that, 'the best in us will want to see all the people living within the boundaries of this parish of Datchet on good terms with one another'. Great fun was had by the procession, led by the vicar and Mr. Page as chairman of the parish council, followed by children, carrying the stakes and poles, as well as many other residents. Only one

stake from the previous beating was found, at the Myrke. Hedges and ditches made the route difficult, but a real boundary problem was discovered at Sunnymeads, where half a dozen bungalow owners were politely informed that they lived in Datchet parish and not Wraysbury. Apart from geographical reasons, this was significant because rates were due to the relevant parish council and services would be expected in return. The beaters had found the round trip much longer than they had expected, and they were 'freely spattered with mud' by the end. The occasion was rounded off by a dinner at the *Manor Hotel*, where speeches were made thanking and praising the parish council, Lord Montagu's representative, the fire brigade and the press. A film was made of the day, which was later seen at the cinema in Windsor with great excitement.

At all village occasions from 1887, including unveiling the war memorial and beating the bounds, the volunteer fire brigade was a necessary part of the proceedings until it was superseded, first by the district and then by the county fire service in 1947. The brigade was very efficient, proud to have reached a fire at Edward VII hospital before the Windsor unit arrived. During the war years there was a great fire at the old G.W.K. works in Holmlea Road, where Kinross had stored hay to save making ricks. The firemen had to collect their horses which were grazing in a field off the Slough Road, so by the time they got there all the buildings were ablaze and there was little they could do. However, they did rescue four horses from a stable by putting sacks over their heads and forcing them out through the intense heat. The weather was extremely cold, so that water

101 Beating of the Bounds, 1925. The men in uniform are the fire brigade, holding the pole is Mr. Page, and fourth from right is John Kinross. The seated figure dressed in 1904 costume is 'Tinny' Elmes, the postman. Old Captain Cleversley can be identified by his white beard.

102 Fire brigade with 'The Lady Aird' engine, 1930s.

103   Coronation arch at the top of High Street, built and painted by Mr. Masters and Mr. Avis.

leaking from the hoses turned to ice and the captain, old George Cleversley, had icicles dripping from his beard. The Cleversley family, George the father and his four sons, who formed a major part of the brigade, were also builders and undertakers with workshops on the site of the modern Post Office and W.I. Hall. Their Chief Officer, James Hale Pearce, was also a builder, one of the last representatives of the Hale family who owned Church Cottage. (By this time the corner house was a grocer's, later the International Stores, and Thomas Hammerson had taken over the smith's business, re-establishing it near the *Morning Star*.) Although they had already been given a steam appliance, in the 1920s the brigade became the proud owners of a motor fire engine, bought by Sir John Aird of Churchmead House, and named 'The Lady Aird'.

During the 1920s two more places of worship were built in Datchet, the Catholic Church in Eton Road and the Christian Brethren's Gospel Hall in Horton Road. The Catholics first established a boarding school or seminary on land bought in 1923 by Lord Braye who had founded Our Lady of Sorrows at Eton in 1915. The school had its own small chapel but the church itself was built in memory of Lord Braye by his widow in 1928, and is part of the joint parish of Eton and Datchet. The school is now used as a priest's house and a parish hall, while a nursing home has been built in the central part of the grounds. The Kiltegan Fathers now run the English head-quarters of St Patrick's Missionary Society from there. The Christian Brethren of Windsor founded a new branch in Datchet in the early 1920s, the first mission hall being in Penn Road.

This was replaced in about 1930 by a wooden building on the same site as the present Gospel Chapel, near the old gravel pit in Horton Road. The Brethren and their well attended Sunday School were led for many years by Mr. Avis and his wife, who were much respected in the village. He was the local sign writer and also built a model of Datchet village on land by White's Lane in Slough Road, near where he lived.

Mr. Avis's talents were dramatically evident at the coronation of George VI in May 1937, together with those of Mr. Nelson Masters the builder. Overnight, a grand 'stone' arch sprang up where none had been before across the top of the High Street. There was a widespread tradition of celebration arches (one was built at Ditton Park gate for Queen Victoria's Golden Jubilee), but this was the first in the village itself and it caused great excitement. The dairy shop next to it also acquired

a thatched roof and the first event of the day was an inspection of the decorated houses. Then there was a carnival and sports on the cricket field, tea in a series of sittings to accommodate everybody, and dancing on the village green until midnight. There were also river sports, including lilo races, boxing on rafts and a mid-river powder fight, followed by a procession of illuminated boats after dark.

A little further down the river, on the site of Evelyn Ellis's Rosenau House, the fashionable Pavilion Club had been built in 1931 by Martin Poulsen, formerly the head waiter at the Embassy Club in London. There was an air of scandal about what went on there, and its private approach by boat was appreciated in particular by two people who did not want their meetings to be made public, the future Edward VIII and Mrs. Simpson. Vera Lynn sang there, and it was a magnet for 'fast' London society, including the Mitford sisters

104   The Pavilion Club, on the riverside site of Rosenau house, 1930s.

and the Duke of Kent as well as film and theatre stars, a clientèle which also frequented the Café de Paris where Poulsen himself was killed by a bomb in 1941. The club had a sliding roof over the central dance floor which opened completely to the sky, and electric canoes which could be brought right up to the building. In 1935 there was a spectacular fire there, fought by the Datchet brigade as well as those from Windsor, Slough and Eton, and though much damaged the building did survive and still exists as a private house. Many people connected with film and stage lived in Datchet, including Charles Killick at the Manor House, Valentine Dyall, Billy Cotton and Louis Levy, both bandleaders, and Laura LaPlante who lived at Datchet House. (She had the top storey of the house removed and the roof lowered, for unknown reasons.) In more recent times Billie Whitelaw and Sir Donald Pleasance have maintained the theatrical connections of Datchet, which is still, as it always was, a pleasant village within convenient reach of London. A rather more scandalous secret was the presence of Radclyffe Hall (the author of *The Well of Loneliness*), who lived in Queen's Road with her female lover in about 1920.

The more ordinary population of Datchet was changing between the wars, partly due to the employment offered by the Admiralty Compass Observatory and the Radio Research Station at Ditton Park, the first local jobs to be available apart from agriculture and the 'service' trades. Such families as these needed modern houses to buy, and opportunities to build were provided by the owners of Datchet's formerly grand houses, now uneconomical to live in and maintain. In about 1930 Leigh House was demolished and the whole estate was sold off as building plots for houses between the London and Horton Roads. All, that is, except for a green island in Leigh Park, which was Lady Mabel Cholmondeley's cats' cemetery and which she required to be preserved. The Barker family (no relation to Robert) had bought Riding Court from Kinross in 1930, and sold

much of the land to Cranebridge Estates who built houses along the London Road and created Montrose and Fairfield Avenues. Leigh House's neighbour, the Lawns, was not pulled down, but the owner, Frederick Levorno Sabatini, converted the original house into flats and built himself a bungalow in the gardens. The rest of the grounds were bought in 1935 by the building developer, George Scott, who built the Lawn Close estate there. The war prevented the planned developments being completed, and afterwards much of the land opened up in these new extensions to the village was used to build council housing.

Frederick Sabatini had also built a Tudor-style house with a thatched roof, now called Lynton Chase, on the edge of the Lawns' grounds facing Horton Road, using old timbers which may have come from original parts of the Lawn house. In 1941 this house was the scene of a fire which is still remembered as 'the most exciting thing to have happened in Datchet'. The roof burned out completely, although the rest of the building survived, and a huge column of smoke could be seen for miles. The fire brigade did not arrive for 45 minutes, when their main objective was to kill the flames before the wartime blackout hour. In the following weeks the fire and the brigade's apparent inefficiency was the talk of the district, and even the subject of a BBC radio lampoon about village firefighters, but eventually the brigade was exonerated from blame, if not from ridicule. It appeared that the family's nanny had taken the children out to safety and then, with the help of neighbours, started to save valuables, but no one had actually called the fire brigade. The old voluntary brigade was by then under the control of Eton Rural District Council, and was very soon merged with the wartime ARP firefighting services.

Just before the war, the extent and shape of Datchet parish was changed under the Buckinghamshire Review Order. There had been anomalies since medieval times, with the land south of Ditton and west of the Fleet Brook being in a detached part of Stoke Poges. With the Review Order, it was brought into Datchet, but most of the area has now been occupied by the M4 and the reservoir. At the same time, the south eastern loop of the parish beyond Welley Road and containing Kingsmead Farm was absorbed into Horton and Wraysbury parishes. A lake has recently been created at that site as well, following extraction of the gravel.

Modernisation was also due in the church, and the changes were just completed at the outbreak of war. By this time the congregation was much smaller and many of the Victorian pews were removed to create spaces in the outer north aisle for a chapel and a children's corner, and near the south door for a baptistery. All the village's legacies for the poor, which had been administered by the church, were reconsidered by the Charity Commissioners and Datchet United Charities was formed as a result. The funds were combined and the income given, as always, to the needy, in the form of vouchers for food, fuel and clothing. The Barker Bridge House Trustees had a wooden memorial plaque put up in the church to Robert Barker, as his family's marble tablet in the chancel did not record his death or his significance to the village in establishing the Trust.

The Second World War

Almost as soon as war was declared, contingency plans for evacuating children from the cities to the country were put into action, even though there was no immediate danger during the months of the 'phoney war'. By October 1939 two schools from the east end of London, with sundry younger brothers and sisters, were scattered among the parishes of Datchet, Colnbrook, Horton and Old Windsor. The effects on the village school were immediate; the Datchet children attended in the morning and the evacuees in the afternoon, although soon all were accommodated by using the scout hut, the Mission Hall and the Working Men's

Club as classrooms. The cultural collision must have been tremendous, and before long the evacuees were being blamed for all the mischief in the village. Several did admit to damaging trees on the riverside and throwing the six benches there into the river, but it was pointed out that before they arrived the local children were hardly considered to be angels. After the Battle of London in September 1940, more evacuees, mostly mothers and young children, poured into the district and the need for accommodation became desperate as the population increased by over 40 per cent. But safety was not guaranteed here either, and air-raid shelters were being built in many homes as well as at the school.

Slough's factories became enemy targets, and the first war casualty in the village was Jimmy Hill, of the shop on the Common, who was killed in an explosion at the High Duty Alloys factory in Slough. His brother-in-law was killed in the same incident which was suspected to be due to sabotage. Even nearer was Langley airfield and the Hawker Aircraft Company, where 15,000 Hurricanes were produced during the war, and where many people from Datchet were employed. Smouldering drums of foul smelling oily rags were positioned on the road towards Langley as part of a protective dense smoke screen around the Hawker factory. Also as protec-

105 Hill's shop on the Common in the 1930s with Jimmy Hill on the right.

tion for Langley there was an anti-aircraft gun post situated on the Guards' polo ground in Horton Road, where the old pavilion became the officers' mess. The Royal Artillery requisitioned both Churchmead House and Holmwood House in Slough Road, from where they conducted the anti-aircraft operations. One night a bomb fell on this gun post, severing communications between the control centres, and two motorbike despatch riders sped in opposite directions along Horton Road in the dark with vital messages. Both were following the white line in the middle of the road and both were killed in a head-on collision. Other bombs did fall on Datchet, but there were no further fatalities except a large number of chickens at Riding Court, where the bomb made a great crater behind the house. To the great excitement of the village, especially the children, a German plane which had been shot down in the Great Park was displayed outside the school and could be clambered over at the cost of one penny.

At Ditton Park, top secret work continued to produce compasses for all three services, especially the new remote transmission gyro compass, and the staff there increased to over one thousand. Even more significant was the development of radar at the Radio Research Station in the grounds of Ditton Park, later to become the Appleton Laboratories. Radar was first demonstrated in 1935 by Watson Watt who lived in Datchet, and it was realised how vital a role it could play, so that by 1945 radar was described as 'the most decisive weapon of the war'. From the beginning of this war, the population at home was acutely aware of the threat of invasion and

106 Datchet's Home Guard at Windsor Castle with the Queen and Princesses Elizabeth and Margaret, probably at the end of the war.

107   The Special Police outside Cleversley's workshop, 1937.

108   The anti-aircraft gun post on the Common, 1947 floods.

determined to fight with anything that might come to hand. Early recruitment to the Local Defence Volunteers exceeded all expectations and the War Ministry had to organise and equip them much more seriously than they had intended, soon changing their name to the Home Guard, although they are immortalised as 'Dad's Army'. Volunteers from Wraysbury and Horton were combined with those from Datchet, where the platoon was based, at first under Captain Wilfred Good, and then Captain Hathaway. Their official headquarters was at Churchmead House, though the *Royal Stag* was their unofficial base and Datchet House's stables were also used for storage. Their main duties were to guard vital local points; the Victoria and Albert bridges, which were used for troop and tank movements, and the water pumping station in Pocock's Lane. There was also a Special Section of the Home Guard patrolling the Thames between Old Windsor and Romney locks, manned by those who owned their own boats, including Mr. Killick of the Manor House.

109 Datchet cricket team, 1930. Captain Killick is in the front row, wearing a striped blazer; on his right is Mr. Soden, with the hat; E.W. Page is on the far right and Mr. Keer, parish clerk, is second from is next to him on the right.

110 Billingsgate fish market on North Green during the war.

Local fund-raising was often for specific and tangible targets, the Spitfire Fund particularly catching the imagination of the children, one of whom made a model plane to surmount the school's collecting box, which raised the huge sum of £50. Children's activity was also harnessed in the autumn of 1942, when they gathered five hundredweight of conkers to be sold for the production of glucose, and many senior boys and girls were sent to help with crucial agricultural work. For a time, traders from Billingsgate fish market came out to Datchet, a relatively safe place with easy access, where their vans occupied the North Green and Slough Road. The problem of feeding the swelling community at a time when mothers were employed in war work all day led to the first provision of school meals at the Scout Hut. At the same time, infants' nutrition was improved by free cod liver oil and orange juice dispensed from the Working Men's Club.

When peace was declared there were immediate spontaneous celebrations, the church bells ringing after the broadcast was heard, and crowds gathering on the Green in the evening around an enormous bonfire outside the school. On the following days there was a torchlight procession and dancing on the Green, the village was decorated, buildings floodlit, and Victory tea parties were given for the children. A special service was held on the next Sunday, when the church was filled to capacity, and as people came out they cheered the King and Queen who were just then driving past on their way to the service at St Paul's in London. The total of men killed on active duty was 26, just half the number who fell in the First World War, but many families had to wait for the safe return of prisoners from the Far East. Fifteen did return, but the Lewin family made the sad discovery that their son John, from whom they had recently received postcards, had in fact died two years earlier from cholera. The urge to commemorate those killed in this war was not felt as it had been after 1918, and in common with most other places no new memorial was erected. Although plans were being discussed in 1947 to record the deaths on the obelisk on the Green, it was not until 1990 that a plaque was placed on its base by the British Legion.

By the end of the war, significant social changes had taken place in the village. Everybody, regardless of wealth or class, had been affected by extreme shortages and privations; those with cars were forbidden to waste petrol, and those with large houses had them filled with evacuees or troops. Almost all adults were involved in paid or voluntary work, and the supply of servants dried up; those who had depended on them had to learn to cook for themselves. The 'wartime spirit' prevailed everywhere, while in this community patriotic duty also forced change which began to blur the old distinctions between traditional social classes.

The Post-War Years

During the terrible winter of 1947 the war-time community spirit was in action again. After a long period of freezing weather, the thaw brought floods in the Thames valley on a scale not seen since 1894, but not actually as severe as that great flood had been. On the afternoon of Sunday 16 March, a torrent of water came surging down across the Greens from the direction of Slough Road, inundating the village and virtually cutting off Datchet from the outside world. Sumptermead Bank had been breached and the village's defence was gone. Only that ancient bastion of high ground on which the church had been built stood clear of the water, allowing rescue operations to be conducted from the foot of London Road, which was the only remaining access at all passable. The vicarage telephone, one of the few still working, was used to co-ordinate relief and a headquarters was established in Datchet House for the police, firemen, Parish Council, Rural District Council, the Red Cross, W.R.V.S. and the school meals service to evacuate people and feed them. James Cottages opposite the church

111 1947 floods: looking east towards Church Cottage and the International Stores. Rescue operations were conducted from the higher ground at the start of London Road. *Daily Graphic* photograph.

112 1947 floods: looking down the railway line towards Windsor.

113 1947 floods, Montagu Road.

formed a shopping centre, while army DUKWs and lorries ferried supplies and rescued the stranded. As the waters began to subside the vicar, Canon Russell Potter, wrote, 'During this memorable week there has been a truly remarkable expression of cheerfulness under difficulties, readiness to help each other, friendliness and sympathy for those who have suffered most'.

The flood completely surrounded the house called Eton End, whose field backed onto Sumptermead bank where the P.N.E.U. school

(Parents' National Education Union), had just moved to the house from its original rooms at Eton vicarage. It had been established there in 1936 for the children of Eton masters by Miss Frances Johnstone, who had to be rescued from her new school by boat, and in her swimming costume as she had been preparing to make her own escape. There had been a long tradition in Datchet of small private day and boarding schools, but this is the only one which has become a permanent and flourishing institution.

The 1950s saw some of the first improvements to public amenities in the village since the Victorian era. Most significantly, the huge field south of Horton Road was bought in 1950 to provide a recreation ground and thus saved for the future as one of Datchet's defining features. Originally part of the great open Marshfield, it had more than once been put on the market as a site for a housing estate, but was compulsorily purchased under the post-war provision for playing fields. It did not then include the strip of land on the road side of the old ditch, which still belonged to the Sabatini family as owners of the Lawn and had been used as allotments during the war. Until recently, access to the new recreation ground was only from Green Lane, where the entrance gate is still situated but has little function. A plaque beside the gate records the dedication of the ground to E.W. Page and the official opening by Princess Margaret in June 1951. Another of Mr. Avis's triumphal arches appeared for this occasion, standing rather strangely in the middle of the field. Two years later he designed a 'stone' monument on the Green, topped by a huge crown, to mark Queen Elizabeth II's coronation.

In 1948 a Datchet branch of the Women's Institute was founded, at first meeting in the school as many village societies did. There was by then a great need for a modern village hall to serve a population of over three and a half thousand, the Working Men's Club having been built for a village of half that number. However, it was the W.I. which first obtained their own hall, due to the generosity of George Scott, who was impressed by their enthusiasm and resourcefulness. He had bought for

114   Princess Margaret at the opening of the playing fields, 1951; on the right is Charles King, chairman of the parish council, and on the left is Major Soden of The Hall.

redevelopment a group of largely derelict properties between the school and the Manor House, and in 1955 he built the Post Office and a shop with an archway between them leading to a new meeting hall. Although dedicated to the Women's Institute, this hall was used by many other organisations so that it became a village hall in all but name. Also in 1955 the Baptists finally achieved their goal of moving away from the noisy and cramped site near the railway. The plot of land in London Road on which their new chapel was built had been bought from George Scott in 1939, and they had been strenuously raising the funds to build on it since then. The old chapel in the High Street was not demolished but sold for conversion into three shops with flats above.

Although the 1944 Education Act made provision for secondary modern and technical education alongside the grammar schools, Datchet was one of the many places where an all-age school continued to cater for children up to the age of 15 who were not 'selected' to go elsewhere. The delay here was prolonged and serious, partly due to the hope that a Church of England secondary school could be provided to serve Datchet, Horton, Wraysbury and Eton. A site on the road to Horton was earmarked for the purpose in 1938, but by 1954 there had been no progress made as the costs were too high. In that year, children over 13 were transferred to Slough Secondary School in Ragstone Road as an emergency measure. Local children were at a great disadvantage by remaining in the village school, as well as placing an enormous pressure upon the school itself. Eventually, in 1959, Churchmead Secondary School was built in the grounds of the demolished Churchmead House by Buckinghamshire County Council and the old village school re-opened for five to eleven year-olds only. Soon after, in 1960, a new village hall was also opened at Churchmead School, paid for by both the county and the parish council.

115 Temporary monument built on the Green for the Coronation festivities, 1953.

From the 1960s to the Present

During the 1960s greater changes took place in and around Datchet than at any other time since 1850. Some, such as the M4 motorway, were imposed from outside but there were also active forces within the village working for improvements and solutions. In 1961 the Charities Commission established new schemes for the old Barker Bridge House Trust, which still owns the *Royal Stag*. Part of the Trust's land at Southlea was compulsorily purchased during the building of the reservoir and another plot sold for housing, which helped to increase the income. The Trust was reorganised into two separate entities each with its own trustees; two-fifths of the income being for repairs to the church and the remainder, the non-ecclesiastical branch, for the general benefit of the inhabitants. This money was at first spent on general village maintenance through the parish council, but in recent years the funds have been applied as grants to specific community projects.

By 1964, the M4 motorway had been carved through the northern parts of the parish, skirting Ditton Park and Riding Court and isolating both from the village so that their ancient significance to the community is no longer apparent. The old hamlet of Ditton with its Green was obliterated, and the lodge to Ditton Park on the London Road was left stranded in a patch of woodland at the top of Ditton Road, where brickwork can still be traced. Ditton Road itself has been cut through, so that it now appears to have no relation to Ditton Park at all. The motorway has also prevented the spread of housing to the north, virtually squashing the village between the road and the river. Its approach roads caused major reorganisation at the east and west ends of the parish, and in particular gave the name 'The Myrke' to the old Slough end of Datchet Road which had become a cul-de-sac. This had previously been a local and ancient but unofficial field name. The extension of London Road towards the motorway junction was re-named Majors Farm Road from the tenant of Ditton Farm at the time. However, the disruption would have been worse if the projected service areas both north and south of the motorway at Datchet had not been determinedly opposed by the village and by the powerful Residents' Association of the time.

Road traffic was causing other problems in the village, which, with two level crossings and two Thames bridges, could hardly have been in a worse position to cope with it. The Albert Bridge to the south had already been rebuilt in 1920, and by 1963 the Victoria Bridge approach to Windsor had to be closed as it was unsafe. The military vehicles which had used this bridge as a main route during the war had probably contributed to its deterioration, and it was the army which now came to its temporary rescue. There was little prospect of an immediate rebuild as responsibility for the cost was disputed. The South Western Railway Company was held to be liable as it had originally built it during the race to take the line into Windsor station. So, while arguments continued, causing the bridge to be closed for six months, recruits from the Royal Engineers built a girder span over the old structure in five days. It remained in place for three years until the old bridge was demolished and a new one built in 1966. In the same year, the Windsor Relief road was completed, to the great relief of Datchet as it was said to have reduced traffic approaching Windsor through the village by 50 per cent, and eliminated the previous three-quarters of a mile queues at peak times.

The 1960s were also a period of confidence and social activity in the village, perhaps partly due to its people being united against threats from outside. In 1964 Datchet won the Best Kept Village competition for the first time (the second was in 1983), and in commemoration of this achievement Lord Montagu visited two years later to plant an oak tree on the North Green. Then, in 1965, the parish bounds were most memorably beaten once again. On this occasion, the idea was said to have arisen at the *Royal Stag* between Wally Gage of the Cricket Club and Laurie Weaver of the parish council in order to 'get the people of the village together, out of their cliques'. Several hundred people actually walked the bounds, far more than previously, with many in motley fancy dress. Following tradition, 12 boys were beaten at the boundary points, and Albert Lewin walked with the party carrying a leaping pole which his brother had carried at the 1904 beating. It was also said that 2,000 visitors came to Datchet for the day and that 'everyone' who lived in the village was out joining in the fun. From the balcony of the Post House in the High Street, Sonya Middlemass dressed as Nell Gwynn sold oranges to the crowds, and Billie Whitelaw, who lived at Riverside, presented the prizes for the Rustic Regatta, at which the Datchet Players enacted the ducking of Falstaff.

116 Beating the Bounds, 1965: the procession along the High Street.

Afterwards, a huge procession was led by the Datchet Folk Dance Group to an ox-roasting on the recreation ground, followed by dancing at Churchmead and on the Green. While money was raised for charity, the whole day was primarily a social occasion, and as such was a more lasting success than the most recent beating of the bounds in 1987.

Beneath the jolly surface, the less pleasant matter of sewage was reaching a crisis point. The village was still using cess pits which had to be emptied by pumping out; they frequently overflowed and were suspected of causing danger to health (the 'Datchet bug'), as well as a serious nuisance. Although a £1 million scheme had been planned for some years, it fell victim to the government freeze on expenditure. There was also delay due to the objections of the landowners where the pumping station was

planned, and a public enquiry was ordered. Eventually work was begun in 1969, when the excavated Greens were a distressing sight, but in a good cause. Until this time, the only car park was in front of the village school, but in 1969 two larger ones were provided near the station and behind the Cut. The school's 'gossip area' was then created and grassed over to become an extension of the Greens, largely at the instigation of the headteacher at the time, Philip Parsons.

In 1969 Buckinghamshire County Council's Planning Department issued the Datchet Development Plan. This was a highly significant document which assessed the village's problems and potential, and embodied many ideas which the parish council had been discussing for some years. Much of what has taken place since is a direct result of plans drawn

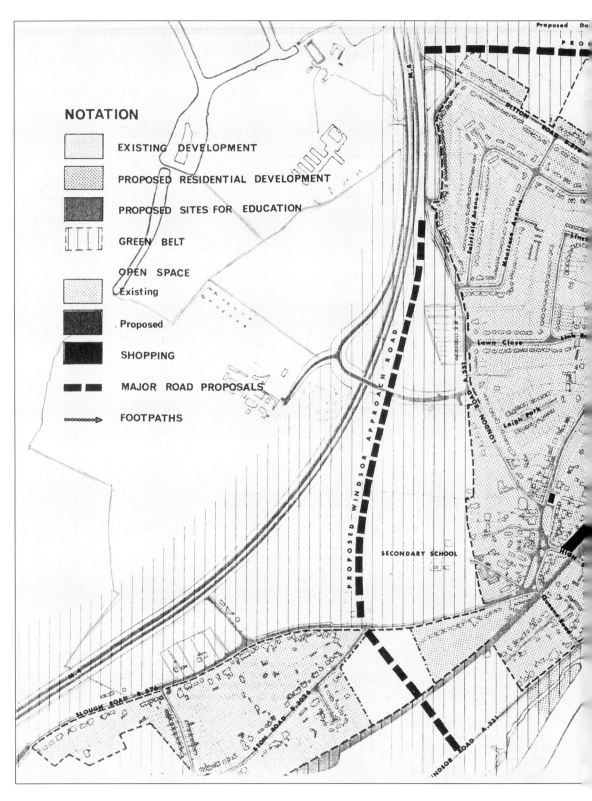

NOTATION

EXISTING DEVELOPMENT

PROPOSED RESIDENTIAL DEVELOPMENT

PROPOSED SITES FOR EDUCATION

GREEN BELT

OPEN SPACE

Existing

Proposed

SHOPPING

MAJOR ROAD PROPOSALS

FOOTPATHS

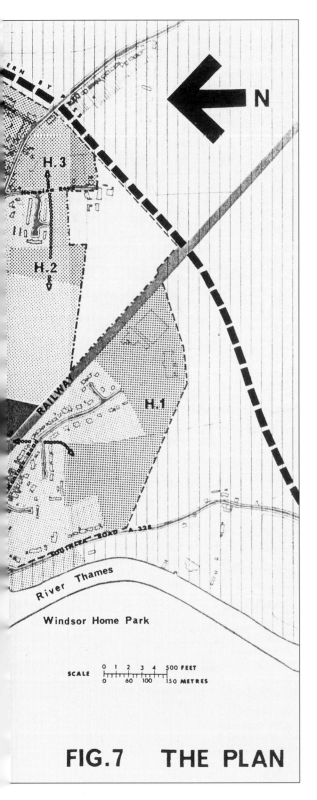

FIG.7   THE PLAN

up then, though the radical by-pass system, which could have solved Datchet's traffic problems for the future, remained on the drawing board. To relieve the village centre, a new railway crossing was considered an absolute priority. It was to be part of a Windsor Approach Road, going west from the M4 junction and continuing the line of Majors Farm Road by skirting south of the motorway across farmland and emerging along the edge of Churchmead's grounds at the present mini-roundabout. From there it would have crossed the site where Ruscombe Gardens has now been built, over the railway by a new bridge and across the golf course to join the Windsor Road. In the longer term, an eastern by-pass was planned, from the top of Ditton Road round the edge of the proposed reservoir, crossing Horton Road and the railway to emerge into Southlea Road just by the farm. This route was named the Bullock by-pass, after the parish councillor who first suggested it. While on paper these proposals seemed ideal and even obvious, there would in fact have been major loss of farmland and objections from all those living near the routes, as well as serious economic obstacles of which the planners were well aware at the time.

Plans were also made for Datchet's growing housing needs, as the population was expected to increase from around 4,500 to 6,000 people. (At the 1991 census it was just below 5,000.) Several overcrowded and derelict areas were identified in and around Green Lane, Holmlea Road, New Road and Penn Road, where it was thought that lower density housing built to higher standards would improve the character of the village. Infill housing was recommended at what is now Agar's Place and as an extension of Montagu Road through to Southlea Road. All these developments have taken place, although not necessarily as envisaged in 1969. In recent years more infill has been allowed, particularly in the extensive

grounds of Victorian houses. Interestingly, this is a reversal of the process by which these grounds were originally created, when warrens of small houses were demolished to open up estate gardens. The wisdom of the past, in not building on the areas most liable to flood, has been replaced by planners' regulations which have not yet been tested by a disaster on the scale of those in 1894 and 1947.

In the plan, part of the station yard was earmarked for an extension to the village school, and a completely new school site was reserved on the recreation ground facing Green Lane, as the primary school population was expected to expand into another building. This did not happen, although the old school was greatly extended between 1969 and 1984, and in 1991 the census showed that there was a relatively high proportion of school-age children in Datchet. The plan also endorsed the parish council's aim to take the scruffy 'Sabatini' land, belonging to the Lawn between Horton Road

and the old ditch, into the recreation ground, which was one of the simplest and most effective ideas for improvement. Although the village hall at Churchmead was only a few years old, it was already too small and the school frequently needed to use it as extra teaching space. Denys Randolph, in a magnanimous gesture, bought the Sabatini land for the village, intending that a much larger hall should be built there, capable of staging the Datchet Players' productions. Funds to build were eventually raised by the sale of Churchmead Hall to the school and of land to the east of the 'rec' for housing. At one stage, the recreation ground was threatened by a proposal to extract the gravel beneath it to raise money, but this was defeated by a village vote. After more than ten years of hopes and plans, the splendid Datchet Hall was opened in 1976. It was designed by the local firm of Edgington, Spink and Hyne who also restored Riding Court Farm as their headquarters. Since then the youth club,

118   Cartoon by Jon.

day centre, library and Randolph medical centre have all been built nearby so that the whole area has become, as originally hoped, a new focus for the life of the village. Very appropriately, the Barker Bridge House Trust contributed to building the vehicle bridge which links these facilities with an extra car park. The Datchet Plan marked the end of Buckinghamshire's responsibility for the village, as Slough and the riverside parishes were taken into Berkshire during the local government re-organisation of 1974.

The Queen Mother Reservoir was still described as 'proposed' in 1969, but planning had been under way since just after the war. The new pumping station, with its network of underground tunnels and new intakes, as well the reservoir itself, was completed in 1975 after just five years' work. Around 500 acres of farm land in Horton and Datchet were swallowed up by the huge construction, including the last piece of the Common to the east of Ditton

Road. The reservoir also displaced the travellers who had settled on the old polo ground, and a new site was provided for them at the end of Mill Place. Water has further obliterated the old landscape towards the Wraysbury border, where gravel extraction at Kingsmead Farm, the Welley and the Fleet meadow has produced the Kingsmead and the Thames Valley water sports lakes.

The threat of flooding is currently topical as the Maidenhead Flood Relief Channel is under construction, creating a waterway parallel to the Thames which will flow into the river at Black Potts on Datchet's northern border. The only guarantee given to the village is that, while the new channel will not protect Datchet, it should not actually increase the risk. However, it will alter the landscape near the boundary and obliterate prehistoric sites which are being excavated and recorded before they disappear for ever. The other major project affecting the whole area is the proposed fifth terminal at Heathrow Airport which can only increase the volume of aircraft noise and traffic congestion in the village. But there are ways in which the centre of Datchet is being protected, as a result of the Conservation Area Statement issued by the Royal Borough of Windsor and Maidenhead in 1995. This defines Datchet's character in historical and visual terms, drawing attention to important trees, open spaces, walls and views as well as the buildings, many of which are separately listed as historically significant. The only real problems identified are the ever-increasing through traffic, parking around the Green and the difficulties of pedestrian access. It is this central area which gives the impression of a prosperous and contented village, but behind the scenes the social situation is rather different. The 1991 census showed that a higher proportion of people were unemployed in Datchet than in the rest of the Royal Borough or in Berkshire, and not far below the national level. And although the numbers in skilled non-manual occupations is high, for unskilled workers the figures are double those for the Royal Borough and exceed both the county and national proportions. The presence of both extremes of the social scale represents continuity rather than change, and is one which has been commented on in both the recent and more distant past.

But surprisingly, given its chaotic traffic conditions and modern housing estates, Datchet still remains both a real village and a special place. Much of its great attraction is due to the Greens and to the survival of so many old buildings in a gentle curve around them, though none is individually of outstanding merit. Datchet probably suffered from traffic jams (though not on a twice-daily basis), during the many centuries when its ferry and bridge were a main route between Windsor and London, so its present problems may actually represent continuity with the past rather than change. This is not to imply that radical change is not needed now; the village is suffocating and deserves to be rescued. For many people Datchet remains a place to live while working elsewhere, but business is booming and two of the original manorial centres are back in action. At Riding Court, the renovated farm buildings are occupied by architects and solicitors and the house itself, empty for years, has recently been transformed by Transaction Technology. Their computer systems now fill a new wing while the house has been restored as prestigious offices. Ditton Park has been saved in a similar way, as Computer Associates are currently developing the site as their European head-quarters, including a programme of conservation to rescue the house, moat and parkland from otherwise inevitable decay. At Southlea the Barkers' and Lascelles' Farm still houses a pedigree herd of cows in a rural setting disturbed only by aircraft. Surprisingly large areas of the parish are still in agricultural use, now protected as green belt land, and although most of the wild flowers remembered by the older villagers have been killed by chemicals, at Ditton Park primroses and bluebells still grow in profusion. The boundaries of the parish are still defined by water, though swimming in the Fleet Brook and skating to school along the frozen Linchfield Brook have been replaced by sailing on the reservoir and water skiing on gravel pit lakes. Villagers still fish in the Thames not far from where Charles II fished; they enjoy the river view where the first inhabitants made offerings to the river gods; and the royal family still travel through Datchet on their way to and from London as they have done since Windsor Castle was built.

Notes

Chapter One: The Riverside Settlement: the Prehistoric Period

1. I am indebted to Phil Catherall for this interim interpretation of the site.
2. Undertaken for Datchet Village Society by Dr. J. Timby.
3. Assessment of this stone for Datchet Village Society by Dr. Ruth Saunders, 1999.
4. David Yates, personal communication.
5. A. Mawer and F.M. Stenton, *Buckinghamshire Place Names* (1925), citing Professor Ekwall. Also K. Rutherford Davis, *Britons and Saxons*, (Phillimore, 1982), who draws attention to the almost identical Latin 'Dacetia' in Nièvre, France, now Décize.

Chapter Two: Ferry and Manor: Medieval Times

1. Text and interpretation based on the Phillimore translation for Buckinghamshire, ed. John Morris.
2. (Arundel) Calendar of Inquisitions Post Mortem, Vol. XVIII
3. Ghyll, *History of Wraysbury, Horton and Colnbrook*, (1862).

Chapter Three: The Royal Village: 16th and 17th Centuries

1. Ashmole's account of the Garter procession as quoted in Tighe and Davis, *Annals of Windsor*, (1858).
2. Geoffrey Fisher of the Conway Library, Courtauld Institute of Art, attributes the following to Edward Marshall: monuments and floor slabs of both Hanbury and John Wheeler, and floor slabs of William Wheeler. His is also the suggestion of Isaac Besnier for Mary Delaune's monument, and the attribution of Katherine Balch's to Joseph Latham.
1. For a comprehensive overview of all the documentation referring to Datchet bridges from 1699 to 1851 I am indebted to Geoffrey Phillips, *Thames Crossings* (1981).
2. Turnpike poisoning story from Maxwell Fraser, *The History of Slough (*1973).
3. Extracts from the Barker Bridge House Trust minutes are quoted by kind permission of the Trustees.
4. C.A. Lubbock, *The Herschel Chronicle* (CUP, 1933).
5. I am indebted to Hester Davenport for information about Perdita and Mrs. Jordan.

Chapter Five: Railway and Revival; 19th and Early 20th Centuries

1. Felix Aylmer, *Dickens Incognito* (1959).
2. From R.R. Bolland, *Victorians on the Thames* (1994).
3. By permission of the *Windsor Express*.

Index

Numbers in bold refer to the page numbers for illustrations